Judicial Activism In India

Judicial Activism In India

Dr. B. S. Tyagi

Srishti
Publishers & Distributors

SRISHTI PUBLISHERS & DISTRIBUTORS
64-A, Adhchini
Sri Aurobindo Marg
New Delhi 110 017

First published in 2000 by Srishti Publishers & Distributors

ISBN 81-87075-48-1
Rs. 145.00

Cover Design by Arrt Creations
45 Nehru Apartment, Kalkaji, New Delhi 110 019
e-mail: arrt@vsnl.com

Printed and bound in India by
Saurabh Print-O-Pack, Noida

CONTENTS

PREFACE

India is passing through her transitional period; so it is not surprising if people change their parties, loyalties and ideologies and do not keep their allegiance to the constitution despite their full faith in the wisdom of its architects. At this turning point even people of sharply differing ideologies strike up alliance with one another without losing theoretical paradoxes. In the cut-throat nature of today's politics nothing is alien or behind the times. In this turmoil everyone has to play his role consciously or unconsciously; there is no way to escape even those who are not directly involved in politics. The judiciary, has decidedly, more role to play in the current period; it has to defy Cicero's statement, "in the midst of arms, law stands mute." Its assumed role of an activist or hyper activist is less meant to set things rightthan to prevent the system from collapsing at a single stroke. It is out to save the situation from getting worse at once. Indeed, it is a mentor who is like a last straw in this morass.

Judicial Activism is no permanent solution to any problem; but a temporary relief. It is a moving spirit which makes the judges more conscious and concerned about the unusual things taking place around them. The High Court of Gujarat has defined judicial activism in relation to the judges- "In fact, the Judges without Judicial Activism can perhaps be described as a flower without colour and fragrance and a vehicle without fuel and wheels which is, unavoidably, a must for any court to be known as a Court of justice, substantial justice and the speedy justice!"[1] Thus judiciary is up and running actively.

Here with my humble submission, I disagree with the court's view; most people mistake the court of law for the court of justice. Perhaps faute de mieux. I contend that no court on earth can do justice simply because justice is not its nature. The earthly court can dispense with law effectively. History bears witness to the fact that the earthly courts, while dispensing with the law of the land, have done great injustice to many great men of the world. The court of Athens did injustice to Socrates when he was tried and condemned to death in 299 B.C. He only uttered, "It is now time to depart-for me to die, for you to live." The court of Jerusalem failed to do justice with Jesus Christ. When Pilate unwillingly pronounced his verdict[2] and Jesus was taken for execution, he said, "Father, forgive them, for they do not know what they are doing." A universal message soaked in justice. The court of France could not do justice with Joan of Arc[3] and she was burned alive in 1431. Her last words came out from the depth of her soul. In the words of G.B.Shaw, "O God that madest this beautiful earth, when will it be ready to receive Thy saints? How long, O Lord, how long?"

1 1997 (2) Cri L,J.P. 3602.

2 Pilate called together the chief priests, the rulers and the people, and said to them "You brought me this man as one who was inciting the people to rebellion. I have examined him in your persence and have found no basis for your charges against him.... he has done nothing to deserve death. Therefore, I will punish him and then release him.

3 She was canonized as St. Joan of Arc in 1920.

Again it failed to render justice to Mahatma Gandhi when he was sentenced to seven years imprisonment by a Bombay High Court.The English judge then said "though he is dutybound to punish the Mahatma as per the law, he would be the happiest man if the Government cancelled the punishment."

In fact, Justice is a matter of soul not of mind or body; justice begins where law ends. Both are close neighbours and have their own distinct ambit. A court is chiefly concerned about 'Rule of Law'. The cases with which the court deals, are the cases of the breach of law; they have hardly anything to do with justice. If the case is complicated, the law is re-interpreted and then it is decided within the ambit of the constitution. In this way the court dispenses with law quite conscientiously. All the accused of the multi-crore hawala case have been discharged with the scrupulous observation that there is not an "iota of independent evidence." Of course the Apex court has clearly dispensed with the law; it may be justice for the accused but glaring injustice for the people of the counrty who are still anxious to know where the large sum of Sixty-five Crore rupees has gone; if the accused are innocent. Certainly, the court of justice has no answer. Similarl, is the fate of the persons-both politicians and bureaucrats, involved in other scams. No political accused has so far been punished due to the lack of "independent evidence."

God alone can do justice; it is His jurisdiction. He sees the truth but waits.

In fact, the system we had adopted fifty years ago with high hopes and aspirations, has proved a total failure.

Democracy which has been on trial for the last fifty years in India, has failed in its trial. Where nearly fifty percent people are not willing to exercise their right to vote, the very concept of democracy loses its meaning; the remaining fifty percent hardly practise their franchise without fear or pressure. The unruly incidents of "Violence, booth Capturing and Deaths" mar the ethos of democracy and defeat its aims. The Hindustan Times (Feb 24, 1998) has aptly noted in its editorial, "The point is that violence is perpetrated by the politicians and criminals acting in tandem with a definite purpose-that of frightening away the ordinary people who may not bother to re-emerge even if a repoll is held, and terrorising political opponents and party election officials with a show of strength." Surprisingly enough, despite the Election Commission's best efforts for holding free and fair polls; such politician-cum-criminals succeeded in their aims and got elected. And, we have democracy but "Without choice".

Now people have started thinking about a change in the system; many intellectuals as well as institutions have come out with one suggestion or the other. People have seen that even coalition Government, which is an experiment in Indian Politics, has failed and the leaders have thrown cold water on the hopes of the people. The unprecedented incident of coalition Government of U.P. has not only frustrated people but also shocked the country. When the Kalyan Singh Government was toppled on Feb 21, 1998 and Mr. Jagdambika Pal was sworn in as Chief Minister overnight. Had the court not intervened, the matter would have been at its worst. The Apex court directed to hold a composite floor test at a specially convened session. At the same time the court had to warn that 'serious consequences would follow in the event of breach of peace or disturbance during the session.' The court's step has been criticised in some quarters of the intellectuals as "outside the provision of the constitution" but it has surely averted a great tragedy. Now it is crystal clear that the patch work in the system will not work. It has to be changed-nay, a drastic change into the things not on the surface of the things is required.

It must be kept in mind that no system should be imposed on the people in haste. People should pave the way themselves for the new system according to their need and nature. Let the country bear birth-pangs to give birth to a healthy system. When the time is ripe, the system will spring up. Pre-mature birth to any system would be faux pas. The next ten years will be of great turbulence; many new things will change; many old and shaky ones will be out of the scenario. We should be mentally ready for the change. Let us watch and wait for what is in the womb of time.

Much has been written about judicial activism, much requires to be written and much more will be written in the years to come since the Court is breaking fresh ground in its every judgement. So I do not claim to pass a judgement on its role in the present precarious situation as some are raising their eyebrows over "an excessively independent role" of the judiciary. I have made a humble attempt to bring its role into the lime light. Of course, it is doing more than its assigned role but surely it is not unexpected or unwise. Denying the charge, Justice M.M. Punchhi has said, "We do not run our show for fame, we carry it in as per the constitution." In this task I have been helped by several enlightened persons. It is not possible for me to mention all those names. However, I would like to express my gratitude to Prof. Dr. K.C. Gupta, former Head, Dept. of Political Science, Meerut College, Meerut who discussed many points at length in the new light. I am immensely thankful to my erstwhile Prof. Shri J.P. Savita, Dept. of English, S.D. College, Muzaffar Nagar, who has ever been the sheet anchor to me in the state of confusion both in language and content. I must express my heartiest thanks to Shri Tajendra Kumar, Advocate, former Chairman, Bar Council of U.P. who found valuable moments to go through the manuscript and gave precious suggestions which have been thankfully incorporated.

My thanks are due to other intellectuals whose articles and letters have appeared in several newspapers as well as journals. Several scholarly articles have proved helpful in understanding the different aspects of judicial activism. Besides, the editorials as well as news analysis have given me a right approach to look at the topic from a critical angle. Hence, heartiest thanks to the editors and other persons involved in the paper for making it more informative and enlightening.

CHAPTER ONE

The Indian Political System

The Constitution we adopted in 1950, was not the product of revolution but of a high standard research work after "rqnsacking all the known Constitutions of the world". Hence, most of its provisions were borrowed from the constitutions of other countries. Thc fathers of our Constitution had taken the best out of these constitutions and modified it to suit the cult and culture of our pluralistic society. It was fairly expected to meet the challenges of the time. Being the most lengthy and detailed Constitution of the world, it has mentioned powers and functions of each wing of the Government — legislative, executive and judiciary, in detail. The Constitution has laid down all possible provisions to ward off any confrontation between two organs of the Government. These provisions are meant for the safe and fair of 'infant democracy' in India. It has given us an indirect democratic system which means that the country will be ruled by the people through their representatives. Hence, supremacy of parliament is the essential feature of our political system. In a democratic system, judiciary has a role of vital importance, so an independent and powerful judiciary is one of the salient features of the Indian Constitution.

The Constitution provides that there shall be a Supreme Court of India. In a federal form of Government an independent judiciary must exist for fair and smooth governance. It has been endowed with the power of saying the final word in the moments of crisis. Besides, the Supreme court acts as the guardian and the protector of the Constitution. It keeps an eye on the two wings of the Government to see if they function according to the provisions of the Constitution. The supreme Court protects the Fundamental Rights of the individuals by issuing writs. It interprets the Constitution and prevents the Parliament from enacting any legislation against the spirit and letter of the Constitution. A mention has been made of the whole hierarchy of the judicial system of the country in order to lend a unifying colour to the entire system. The Indian courts of law adjudicate all laws with some interpretation whether in the Centre or in the State. In present times of crises the courts have shown their mettle; they are true to their word and are discharging their assigned duty conscientiously. They enjoy 'a respected reputation for creativity and ingenuity,' they are fully aware of every situation which casts a burden on them greater than ever before.

Judicial Review

Judicial review can be defined, "as the power of a court, to hold unconstitutional and hence unenforceable, any law, official action based on a law, or any other action by a public official, that deems to be in conflict with the basic law, that is the Constitution'[1]. In fact, judicial review, keeps the judge dynamic for the cause of justice-justitia omnibus.

1 The Indian Advocate: Vol. XXVI; 1994-96 (Part 1) P. 35-36

It breathes new life into the old and musty chambers of law (which suits to law of life.) Hence, a sine qua non for a just and civilized society. The Indian Constitution which has conferred the power of judicial review on the Apex Court of India though the constitution has not mentioned the term "judicial review" anywhere. But, the power of judicial review lies in several provisions of the Constitution. Article 13, for example, bears the marginal heading "Laws inconsistent or in derogation of the Fundamental Rights". It is clear that if Parliament passes any law which is inconsistent with the Fundamental Rights it will be scrutinised by the Supreme Court. The second clause of the same Article has prevented the State from making any law which takes away or bridges the rights conferred by that part, and if any such law is made, it shall be void to the extent of the contravention. "Law" includes as per clause (3), any ordinance, order, bye-law, rule regulation, notification, custom or usage. Now, who is going to determine all this? Of course, none but the Supreme Court. Again Article 254 has laid down that in case of inconsistency between laws made by Parliament and laws made by the legislatures of States on subject of the concurrent list, the laws made by the latter stand void to the extent of repugnancy with the laws of the former. This can be decided by the Supreme Court only. Thus, the power of judicial review of the supreme Court is very much a part of the Indian political system.

The Indian Constitution consists of all essential requisites for the exercise of judicial review — as a written and rigid constitution, the federation having division of powers and fundamental rights. The power of judicial review enables the Supreme Court to review the acts and orders of the Legislative and Executive wings of the Government. If they are challenged and are found inconsistent with the Constitution, the Apex Court can declare them void. The Supreme Court also curbs both of the wings of the Government if they go beyond the limits of their authority laid down by the Constitution. They are reminded of their limitations at the same time, and are, thus, directed to act within their ambit for fair and smooth administration. It is also done without any pride and prejudice in the interest of people and the Government as well.

The system of judicial review prevails better in a country where there is a federal constitution because the power of the Government is divided between the federation and the federating units. The Supreme Court has to decide disputes under the power of judicial review. This system is essential for fundamental rights; if these rights are under threat, the Supreme Court is called upon to interfere for their defence. The Supreme Court should also see that what the people are guaranteed by the Constitution, should be enjoyed freely by them. The power of judicial review, thus, helps people to live graceful and dignified lives.

Balance Between Judicial Review and Parliamentary Supremacy

A complete harmony between judicial review and parliamentary supremacy is an outstanding achievement of the architects of the Indian Constitution. The doctrine of an absolute balance of powers between the different wings of the Government is not feasible. Practically, someone must be empowered with having the final say in the matter of disputes. This is the reason that the system of separation of powers in the Constitution of America has failed in real practice. The judiciary in America has its dominance over other organs of the Government under the power of interpretation of the Constitution. Due to this domineering tendency, it is known as 'safety valve' or the `balance wheel' of the Constitution. Chief Justice Hughes has aptly remarked, "The constitution (of the U.S.A.) is what the Supreme Court says it is." It has the power to declare a law null and void passed by the legislature even on the ground that it is not consistent with the general principles of the constitution. Thus, the American judiciary can poke its nose into the legislative policy like a third chamber or super-chamber of the legislature.

In England ,Parliament is supreme. It is free to do what it pleases. Every wing of the Government has to heed what parliament says or does. Blackstone has rightly described the might and majesty of the British Parliament, "it can do everything that is not naturally impossible." That is why the British judges refuse having any power "to sit as a court of appeal against Parliament".

With a view to avoiding either extreme the Indian Constitution has adopted a golden mean between the supremacy of American judiciary and the supremacy of

British parliament. If the judiciary rides the high horse and behaves arrogantly, the Parliament can bring an amendment in the Constitution. Pandit Nehru has rightly described this unique feature of the Indian Constitution, "No Supreme Court, no judiciary, can stand in judgement over the sole will of Parliament, representing the will of the entire community. It can pull up that sovereign will if it goes wrong, but, in the ultimate analysis, when the future of the community is concerned, no judiciary can come in the way. ... Ultimately, the fact remains that the legislature must be supreme and must not be interfered with by the court of Law in such measures as social reforms"[1].

Moreover, the Indian judiciary has stood by the people through thick and thin. It has ever paid due regard to the "sovereign will" of the people but during emergency its wings were clipped and left it in trauma through 42nd Amendment but afterwards in the regime of the Janta Government it was restored to the pre-1976 position to a great extent. Now, it has gained ground by declaring itself judicial review as a basic feature of the Constitution. It has helped the court to cover a wide range of judicial activities to do "complete justice". As S.B. Jai Singhani says, "Under Article 142 of the Constitution, the apex court was given an extraordinary power of the widest amplitude to pass any decree or make any order as was considered necessary for doing complete justice in any cause or matter pending before it— no matter whether the ordinary

1. Basu Acharya Dr. Durga Das, Introduction to the Constitution of India; Prentice Hall of India P. (Ltd.) also Delhi, 1994, P.39.

law of the land provided for such a measure."[1]

The Concept of Judicial Activism

Judicial Activism is a comprehensive term; it encompasses the entire spectrum of the judicial phenomenon. The very basic principle of the judiciary is to ensure justice as well as rule of law for the realization of the noble ideals mentioned in the Preamble— "Justice-social, economic and political." It is a double-edged weapon; it is both-boon and a bane. The whole matter depends upon one's outlook. To the advocates of Judicial Activism it is a "normal assertion of judicial power, a part of judicial review and to uphold rule of law and canons of justice" but on the other hand, to its critics, its is an "abuse" which can spell havoc. Hence, in the light of its power and position enshrined in the Indian Constitution let us discuss the term "Judicial Activism." Two roles of judiciary have been observed-traditional and modern. The traditional role of judiciary has been "to act as umpire, to ensure that limits were observed—especially in a federal distribution of power-and that the citizen's rights were not violated. As the first Chief Justice of India, Justice Hira Lal Kania observed at the inaugural sitting of the Supreme Court of India on 28 January 1950 : "It is not the function of the court to supervise or correct the laws passed by the legislature. The court tries its best to do justice between the parties but if a clear provision exists, it has to administer the law not make a new one".[2]

1. Article in the Indian Express: Dec.23,1996.
2 The Indian Advocate; Vol. XXVII 1996-97, P.2.

Really, it is judicial review in its most refined manner. It is mandatory for the judiciary. If a case comes before the court, it has to pronounce its judgement without the slightest feeling of malice or ill-will to either party. Hence, complete detachment. Mostly, such judgement is based on the letter of the law; to carry out the court's order is the business of the executive and the concerned court bothers little about it. It is well defined by the constitution and accepted in society. In its traditional role the judiciary is, in the words of Francis Bacon, "to interpret law and not to make law." The judgement of the court is based on the interpretation of the "plain and unambiguous" language of law with least care for its far-flung effects on the chamber of the court. The courts in India, too, in the beginning, have adopted the role of "interpreting law" and have avoided any criticism of overriding its ambit. Its stand is, in most of the cases, to stamp on the legislature. Thus, a limited one. The judges hardly intend going beyond their judicious interpretation of law. Truly, it is the traditional colour and culture of the judiciary.

On the other hand, during the past two decades, the Indian judiciary has shed its traditional mantle and has appeared in a new light. Consequently, a new trend has emerged which is "the conscious exercise by judgement of the power of judicial review to meet the changing needs of time." With his approval and appraisal of this new role Justice Michael Kirby, Justice of the High Court of Australia, has observed "Many decisions of the Supreme Court of India show that Court's facility in the development and adaptation of the common law to the enormous contemporary problems and opportunities of India. Those who trouble to examine the law of India carefully soon come to an understanding of the way in which the Supreme Court has, by a series of landmark judgements described by some as "Judicial activism", established basic principles which deserve wider attention."[1] A judicious judge does not like to be mired in the past but he wants to bring out desired results in precarious situations so that people's faith in the wisdom of the judiciary does not shake. To quote A.G. Noorani, "A wise judge is one who heeds the limit on judicial power and judicial function, yet is ingenious and courageous to mould the law, case by case, to answer to the needs of the times the law is not broken, it is evolved".[2] Such judgements, besides the spirit and aim of jurisprudence, involve judiciousness of a judge. It shows the judge best at work. Under this role, the court evolves new perceptions in accordance with the exigency of the matter. Here the court traverses the walls of hoary traditions and explores new horizons. Though it appears alien to the set principles of law, it is wholly meant to provide relief to the aggrieved and to set the wrong right. In such a new, unexpected situation the court lays down "priorities, policies, and programmes and gives directions to execute them when they are not obligatory and are entirely in the discretion of the executive and the legislature or other authorities." It is quite in consonance with the old maxim that 'it is the proper function of a good judge to expand his jurisdiction.' The court interprets Constitution or statutes with novel ideas to meet the challenges in adverse circumstances.

1 Ibid : P. 13.

2. Span April / May 1997; P. 16.

These interpretations are well founded on the logic of jurisprudence and hit the nail on the head. While interpreting the Constitution, the court breaks new ground and sets new precepts to be followed. It gives new meaning to the old law which is quite capable of having a firm grasp on the situation. Certainly, it is an uphill task; it requires a deep insight into things. For sagacious interpretation and a fresh application of law with novel outlook, the court is often charged with "Judicial Activism."

Judicial Review and Interpretation of Article 142

The interpretation of Article 142 is a great source of deriving wide powers for the Supreme Court. It has been interpreted time and again to meet a new situation. Article 142 (1) reads : "The Supreme Court in the exercise of its jurisdiction may pass such decree or make such order as is necessary for doing complete justice in any cause or matter pending before it..." The language of the Art referred to has no ambiguity but the Supreme Court has reinterpreted it in wider terms in the case of Delhi Judicial Service Association Vs. State of Gujrat (1991 : 3 Sc R 936 at 997) The Court holds : "It may be noticed that in Premchand Garg's and Antulay's case (supra) observations with regard to the extent of this Court's power under Art 142 (1) were made in the context of fundamental rights. Those observations have no bearing on the question in issue as there is no provision in any substantive law restricting this court's power to quash proceedings pending before a subordinate court. This court's power under Art 142 (1) to do "complete justice" is entirely of a different level and of a different quality. Any prohibition or restriction contained in ordinary laws cannot act as a limitation on the constitutional power of this court. Once this court has is in of a cause or matter before it, it has power to issue any order or direction to do "complete justice" in the matter. This constitutional power of the Apex Court cannot be limited or restricted by provisions contained in statutory law." Thus, the court has made it quite clear that it is nothing beyond its ambit if it issues direction to do "complete justice" under a new situation.

While interpreting the Constitution or statutes the Court has always upheld the old adage that none is above the law. The interpretations made by the courts, have introduced certain innovations enlarging fundamental rights in the areas which were not thought of earlier such as protection of environment. Environmental pollution is hazardous for people's health; here right to life is violated by not protecting the environment. Polluted air poses danger to human existence; as the latest report reveals, Delhi is the most polluted city in the world where every third child is prey to asthma. To safeguard the right to life the court has to ban the felling of trees. Certainly surprising but an innovation. Again, when the Supreme Court declared, "Telephone tapping violates right to privacy"; it was a prescient interpretation of Article 19(1) (a) of the Constitution in which the right to freedom of speech is mentioned. In fact, the Constitution does not mention or guarantee the right to privacy in clear cut terms; hence the court had to interpret Article 19 (1) (a) to ensure this fundamental right. Certainly, the judgement came out like a shock for those who intended to abridge the right of an individual. Similarly, the right to life and personal liberty guaranteed by Article 21 was interpreted. The Apex Court ordered the closure of factories situated in Delhi since they caused air pollution. Again, the court's order broke the fetters of about 100 million children who were working in hazardous industries in pitiable conditions. It also directed payment of Rs. 20,000 as "compensation for every child so employed to be deposited in a fund to ensure compulsory primary education". The court directed the State, too, for providing a job for the guardian or parent in place of the child or contribute Rs.5,000 to the fund. The court had to put restraints on the running of saw mills and mining in forest areas where the lives of workers was threatened. Besides, the court has stepped in to defend the rights of individuals guaranteed in the constitution. Truly, the judgements of the court with novel meaning have stunned orthodox minds. To quote Mr. Jagmohan, former Governor of Jammu and Kashmir, "The public, by and large, is happy about this development. In fact, healthy and positive judicial dynamism is nothing but the ability of a creative and constructive court to interpret the laws in such a manner that they answer the need of the hour, provide intrinsic, as distinct from technical, justice and give expression to the latent feelings of the people."[1] At present, the way and style in which the Indian Courts are working show their creativity and logical application of mind which marks the steady progress of jurisprudence. These innovations and initiative are the result of a constructive and positive outlook towards life; it not only strengthens the rule

1. An article in The Indian Express, December 16, 1996.

of law but also enriches human life. Very few judges are gifted with such power of creativity; they make history and explore new horizons for a better life. Such gifted judges do not act mechanicaly; they observe each situation from a fresh angle and act accordingly. Justice cannot be dispensed with bluntly; it requires a fresh application of mind each time.

Last but not the least, the judiciary has ever been active. It has come out "to afford redress to the aggrieved party in case there is violation of fundamental rights and for any other purpose". When the courts pronounced judgment in the political field and the political masters found themselves in the dock, a severe charge was made against the judiciary that it had over-stepped the limits of its authority. There was much hue and cry when the investigating agencies were monitored by the courts themselves "to look into the acts of political corruption and amassment of ill-gotten wealth by political bosses" against whom they could not probe fairly. They could not discharge their duties because they were under their administrative control. The judiciary did nothing contrary to the law by taking supervision of the investigating agencies into their own hands. Justice H.R. Khanna has rightly remarked, "The judiciary, on doing so, has removed the shadow of fear and make the investigating officers to enforce the rule of law so that none may carry the notion that he is above the law.[1] To quote him again, "It is as a result of ensuring the rule of law that many skeletons in the cupboards of ministers and other political high-ups have been

1. Article in Politics India

revealed and acts of amassment of huge amounts of wealth through corrupt means have come to light"[1].

If the courts had to issue directions in administrative matters, it was to face practical difficulties to ensure the rule of law. It was not the usurpation of legislative and executive powers. It was a painful duty which the courts had to discharge just to save the system from collapse. It was imperative for the court to put restraint upon the 'law makers' when they had become "law breakers'. Mr. Bindheswar Pathak gives a vivid description of failure on the part of the administration. "The weakening of administration following loss of surrender of constitutional responsibility by bureaucrats has resulted in an unholy alliance between the criminals and politicians, the result of which is there for all to see. What we see by way of a series of scams, are only the tips of the icebergs; the pervasive corruption, breakdown of law and order. The insecurity of private citizens has destroyed the ability of the democracy to hold the system together.[2] Due to pervasive corruption and immorality in public offices our houses have lost their dignity and decorum. In the words of Dr. Subhash Kashyap, former Secretary General Lok Sabha, "the houses of our legislatures remain silent spectators or are alleged to have become sanctuaries for the corrupt and criminal politicians and escapadoes from law and if the law-makers and rulers do not perform their assigned tasks,

1. Ibid

2. An article in The Hindustan Times, April 28, 1996.

judiciary cannot be blamed for trying to provide in public interest a check and a correction by asking them to follow the law and the Constitution and to perform their responsibilities of governance".[1]

The present approach of the judiciary in India is the result of precarious situations prevailing in every sphere of society. The very notion of justice was jeopardized; the ideals for which the Constitution stands were brutally assailed due to selfish motives. Even responsible persons in both executive and legislative spheres began to dodge the column and the rule of law was meant only for the ordinary men; the court stepped in to set the things right. To quote Justice Ahmadi, "when derelictions of constitutional obligations and gross violations of human rights are brought to the notice of the Supreme Court, it cannot be expected to split hairs in an effort to maintain the 'delicate balance' of power between the wings of Government; it must act and act in a positive manner that will provide relief, which is real and not illusory, to the parties who exercise their fundamental right in invoking its jurisdiction".[2] Thus, the judiciary has come out for the relief of the people in every field wherever it is called upon.

1. An article in Politics India.

2. The Indian Advocate P.39.

CHAPTER TWO

Democracy and Judicial Review

1. Concept of Democracy

If most of the countries in the world have adopted democracy, it is not because it is a perfect system or the best way to lead a contented life but because it is a better system. The term 'Democracy' has been discussed from Plato to the present day by thinkers who tend to think of a better and just society. Hence, we have a wide variety of its connotations; yet it is to be interpreted with the tint of contemporary experience. As democracy aims at establishing a just society, the judiciary is logically and inevitably associated with it. Both are complementary to each other. If democracy prepares the ground to realize lofty ideals of life, the court acts as a sentinel on the 'qui vive'. How judicial review is a watch word when democracy especially in India - a land of religion and philosophy, aims at providing people all good conditions which make life worth-living. For this purpose let us discuss the latest concept of democracy which is a befitting reply to those who wish to put a restraint on judiciary in India which is basically based on the philosophy of justice.

Today the very basic tenet of democracy—that all that rests upon the consent of the governed is just and natural—has been flouted and the power concept has got an upper hand. In the present time the democratic process has cast people into a strange paradox; in fact our democratic system is "the dictatorship of the majority". In this sort of dictatorship public good or welfare has been snowed up and the representatives as well as the officials are blind to the very fact; as the examples of captain Satish Sharma, Petroleum Minister, Mrs. Sheela Kaul and Mr. P.K. Thungon, Ministers of Urban Development, Ms. Jaya Lalitha, Chief Minister of Tamil Nadu, Mr. Sukh Ram, Telecom Minister etc. have shown that they have acted like kings or emperors. Several innocent people have to suffer. Commenting on the misuse of power by ministers, the Supreme Court observes, "When grave illegality of great magnitude is required to be cured, at times a sort of surgery becomes necessary and then suffering cannot be avoided altogether". To set the things right the court had to order the eviction of about 2000 central Government employees who were allotted out-of-turn Government accommodation. The theory and logic of democracy has failed as the judiciary has brought such persons to the dock. As Plato adopts a realistic approach and remarks in the Republic, 'it is not the makers or producers but the users or consumers of things who are the best judges of their values'. Of course, the users have knowledge of the democratic process in which they feel robbed by their own persons. In the light of this bitter experience people suffer from the sordid consequences of democratic dictatorship which are bound to shatter the truth of democracy. If we look into the things, truth or hard reality may appear in Nietzsche's statement, "the democratization of Europe will tend to produce a type prepared for slavery in the most subtle sense of the term."[1]

1 C. L. Wayper, Polictical Thought, p.120.

In a democratic system every citizen is free to act according to the dictates of his conscience but such freedom is not practised even by parliamentarians. They work under the whip of the party and their actions are not free from pride and prejudice; conscience finds no room in their practice. They do not stand up in the house to call right as right or wrong as wrong. Having been confined to their own interests they have no hesitation in pulling down Government without rhyme or reason. People all over the country have witnessed noisy and disgraceful scenes in the Parliament which is no better than pandemonium. During its verdict the court regretfully has gone to the extent of calling Parliament "a fish market." (the comment was dropped out of the record at the Supreme Court's order) Not only the court but also the Lok Sabha speaker P.A. Sangma and many MPs have expressed their anxiety over the declining decorum of the Parliament. People are badly hurt at the unruly behaviour and unparliamentary language used by the MPs and legislators. To quote a letter published in the Hindustan Times (April 21, 1997) "The recent observation of the Lok Sabha Speaker, Mr.P.A. Sangma, that our Parliament is behaving like a Panchayat", was apt and timely. It is indeed a tragedy that in our country erosion of basic democratic values has assumed serious proportions. Time and again the elected representatives have made a mockery of democracy with their unbecoming and undemocratic behaviour on the floor of the House. Sadly, this fissiparous tendency has already done incalculable harm to the unity and integrity of the country. Ironically, enough money and muscle power are being freely used by political parties to achieve their selfish ends with scant respect for well established democratic norms and principles ..." Indeed, these words express the anguish of the millions. When we do not stick to the democratic values how can we claim to be democratic. In every process - from election to the selection of a peon we have become undemocratic and go ahead with little thought of future consequences. We are governed like slaves by one things. Either we do not listen to our conscience or it is suppressed. Even the representatives are in thrall; whether it is a party whip or any thing else it is far from being just. Truly if the democrats do not practise the basic principles of democracy, our system will certainly be out of gear. Dr.Radhakrishnan, long ago, had sensed the danger of undemocratic and narrow attitude and therefore he warned, "We talk democracy but when it comes to any particular thing, we prefer a man belonging to our caste, or community or religion. So long as we have this kind of temptation, it means that our democracy is a phoney kind of democracy".[1] This kind of democracy has been in practice since independence and we are subjected to unworthy and unnatural elements, which are alien to democracy. If democracy is divested of its ideals, Radhakrishnan observes, "that would be dictatorship".[2]

No doubt the working style of our ministers which has come to light, clearly shows that they are dictators in democracy and this wholly unconstitutional and incompatible with the basic faith of democracy.

1. Radhakrishnan's Our Heritage, P.60.
2. Radhakrishnan's The Hindu View of Life P.83.

2. Judicial Review

Now let us discuss judicial review and whether it is compatible with the theory and logic of democracy. In fact, judicial review is vastly comprehensive; it is not vying with the democratic set up. In the light of the above discussion about the practice of democracy, judicial review becomes more logical and necessary for the safe existence of democracy and for the survival of the constitution. When the representative body becomes tyrannical or dictatorial, the judiciary takes up cudgels for the noble cause on cue. That is why the fathers of the constitution preferred the American doctrine of 'limited Government' to the English doctrine of Parliamentary sovereignty. The verdict of the Supreme Court in regard to many cases of public interest has proved the fact that judicial review is a check upon tyrannical and treacherous democrats. As P.A. Sangma has remarked, "Our judiciary has rendered yeoman service in this area. Executive dormancy does trigger off judicial activism. I am afraid if the people of this country find that their aspirations and fundamental rights are not protected because of the State's inaction, they go to the courts. Why blame the courts, it can only be blamed on the undesirable proclivity to acquiescence."[1] For the protection of fundamental rights judicial review is necessary; it has stood by woe-stricken people. The Apex Court has invalidated "a dozen of statutes and a like number of administrative acts on the ground of violation of the fundamental rights."

1. The Hindustan Times, March 9, 1997.

Thus, judicial review, a "basic feature" of our constitution, is a necessity in our system.

We are aware of abuses of democratic power. As Winston Churchill has remarked, "Democracy is the worst form of government. Unfortunately we do not know anything better;" so it is likely the office bearers may go astray. Hence, to prevent and to redress abuse of power judicial review is indispensable in democracy. People in India have become victims of abuses of power during the last five decades. They have been deprived of their due share and the few privileged ones have enjoyed the fruits of the poor people's labour. Referring to the irregularity on the part of an official, the Delhi High Court regretted, "Files of various departments go to the Law Ministry and such a person (Law Secretary) getting an allotment for his relative is very unfortunate." In all departments almost such cases have been brought out which have shaken people's faith in democracy and some people gathered courage to look forward to the court to check the abuse of power. The court was surprised at the findings of such "highly arbitrary, oppressive and unconstitutional" acts. The Supreme Court not only cancelled 14 allotments made by Mr.Satish Sharma, Union Petroleum Minister, from his discretionary quota but also slapped a fine of Rs.50 lakh on him. The Apex Court observed that Mr.Sharma has doled out favours as if "he was a king and the pumps were his personal property". Another Union Petroleum Minister B. Shankranand also did undemocratic acts and alloted LPG, kerosene and petrol dealership to "his cronies and relatives of political bigwigs." Indeed, the favoured or the chosen persons were kith and kin of ministers and senior bureaucrats. These political big shots forgot the welfare of common men and were dictated by selfish desires. To quote an editorial (H.T. April 26, 97) "Discretionary quota has become an aberration which was not its original intention. It was meant to help the needy. But this purpose was forgotten and it became a plaything in the hands of ruling politicians." Of course, such abuses pose a real threat to democracy to which we are wedded. Today people are aware more than ever before, so judicial review is an article of strong faith which strengthens democracy.

Moreover, the judiciary is the guardian of the conscience of the people. In fact judicial power is never exercised for giving effect to the will of the judge but to the will of the law. When a question is in dispute, it is supposed that the judges know better what the will of the law is and they act accordingly to arrive at a decision. A judge is an instrument of the law. When the conscience of the people or the general will is neglected by their respresentatives, it is the court which stands up to guard and to respect the conscience of the people. To quote Justice Douglas, "The Judiciary is in a high sense the guardians of the conscience of the people as well as the law of the land. It is much further removed from the political arena than the administrative agencies or the legislature. It sits aloof and detached from the community, not subject to the stresses and political storms of the other branches. Its decisions are more apt to reflect tradition and first principle than political expediency."[1]

1. We, the Judges New York, 1956, P. 445.

In India when most of the ruling politicians and officials are busy in their own affairs, even at the cost of the interest of the people who send them to the House and the opposition's voice goes unheeded, the judiciary is the only reliable guardian of the conscience of the people. It has ever held the old adage, "Be you ever so high, the law is above you" and undoubtedly, the judiciary has brought many high persons to the dock.

Judicial review is required to fill the vacuum created by the legislature or executive. It is a constitutional obligation of the courts to reduce the gap between law and justice. This 'gap' is a great hindrance in the way of justice. Justice J.S. Verma has observed, "If there is a gap between law and justice, though ideally there should not be any gap, it can be abridged by the court through law itself by using tools of judicial activism and creativity."[1] Here lies the relevance and expediency of judicial review in a democratic system. The gap between law and justice hurts badly the conscience of the people. Law, indeed, finds life in the philosophy of justice which is a virtue to be achieved through the long process of experience. As Justice Holmes has said, "The life of the law has not been logic; it has been experience. The felt necessities of the time, the prevalent moral and political theories, institutions of public policy, avowed or unconscious, even the prejudices which judges share with their fellow men, have had a good deal more to do than the syllogism in determining the rules by which men should be

1. The Hindustan Times, 5th May 97.

governed .... The very considerations which judges most rarely mention and always with an apology, are the secret roots from which the law draws all the juices of life. I mean, of course, considerations of what is expedient for the community government."[1]

This is the accurate judicial process the primary concern is of which the conscience of the community. Law should take its course speedily so that justice may be dispensed to the people as early as possible to save them from the feeling of guilt if the person is innocent. They should not suffer from unnecessary tension or ill reputation due to false and malignant charges. Justice J.S. Verma holds, "It is the duty of the court to ensure that the trials are completed as early as possible so as to ensure that innocent people get a clean chit without any delay." In this field, too, the court has done an excellent job. The Delhi High court quashed the charges against Mr. L.K. Advani and Mr. V.C. shukla in the Hawala case and gave them a clean chit. Following the ruling of the High Court, the lower court of Delhi gave a clean chit to Mr. M.L. Khurana who stepped down from the office of the Chief Minister of Delhi after the charge of his involvement in the Hawala case. The remark of Justice Prem Kumar, a judge in the subordinate court in Delhi is worth quoting, "In the present circumstances when people's expectations and aspirations are being totally ignored by both the legislature and the executive, it is the court which has came to their rescue"[2].

1. The common Law. Booton: Kittle Brown 1981, pp. 1.35.
2. The Hindustan Times, 20th Jan. 97.

In fact, the law decides the course of action and justice adores people's conscience.

The grand edifice of democracy rests on three pillars - the legislature, the executive and the judiciary. Indeed, the judiciary has a key role to play for the smooth and fair running of the system. Directly and indirectly people share power in a democratic Government so that any possibility of a despotic situation may be avoided. All these three pillars are strongly built up assisting one another to attain the goal of establishing a welfare state. The constitution has empowered the trio in their own fields on the doctrine of the separation of power. However, none has uncontrolled freedom to act licentiously or in a nonethical manner. Theoretically in our parliamentary system the elected legislature controls the bureaucracy through the Minister. Parliament expects that the ministers will manage their departments efficiently. They should be fully aware of what is going on in their departments. Hence, they alone are responsible for affairs of the various departments. It is one of the fundamentals of our system of Government that the Minister is responsible to Parliament, and through Parliament to the public for every act of the Executive. In fact, this is a corner stone of our system of Parliamentary Government. Questions can be put to him in the House about the working style of his department. Parliament, thus, spends considerable time in reviewing,scrutinizing and evaluating Public Administration.

In a democracy, it seems that judiciary has more responsibility in its share. It controls administration to ensure the legality of administrative acts and thus protects the rights of citizens against any unlawful use of authority. In modern times the activities of the state are increasing day by day. So, the problem of protecting citizens against the misuse of administrative authority is an uphill task. The rights of the citizens in a democratic state are to be protected against the abuse of authority, partiality and official favouritism. The doctrine of the rule of law which is one of the basic features of our constitution, lays down the basis of judicial control over administrative acts. If the citizens feel that their rights have been usurped by misuse or wrong use of administrative authority, they can knock on the door of the Court for the redress of their grievances. No administrative authority is above law. The judiciary knows well how to meet the needs of the hour. In India during past years many serious problems have arisen but the legislature has failed to face them boldly. Matters of public importance are not discussed properly in the House. They do not seem to have knowledge of how to grapple with ticklish tangles which pose a threat to the solidarity of the country. The Lok Sabha Speaker Mr.P.A. Sangma has expressed his displeasure at the working style of the legislators, "The MPs end up indulging in tedious repetitions, causing breaches of order, unparliamentary expression and disorderly conduct."[1] During discussion the House is completely in chaos and things move in quite an undemocratic way. It seems that there is a free-for-all. The working sittings of the House have declined, too, during past years which is not a healthy sign in a democratic system. Most of its time is spent on the issues which are meant for the state Assembly.

1. The Hinustan Times, March 9, 97.

According to Mr.P.A. Sangma, the Lok Sabha speaker, "An analysis of the work transacted by the Lok Sabha since 1952 reveals that the average number of sittings was 135. However, during the period 1991-95, it had come down to 80........" Again.

"I guess this is again a reflection of the failure of the executive to meet the aspirations of the people. It is taking away the essence of Parliament. Again I am told there are many State Legislators that meet for less than a month in a year. This is astonishing."[1] It is clear that the situation is deteriorating day by day and the ideals and values envisaged by our forefathers are in the cart. Our legislators have failed in discharging their duty honestly; their integrity and probity is in question. Similarly, the executive has turned a deaf ear to the request of the aggrieved persons. As the two organs of the Government have become lethargic, naturally, the third one - the judiciary has to strain extra to make the system workable. The remark of Mr. Ram Jethmalani is worth quoting, "the survival of the Indian Republic was solely due to the independent and positive role played by the judiciary."[2] The failure of the executive and the legislature has been regretted all over the country by the people who are committed to the democratic ideals. Prof. Madhu Dandavate, Deputy Chairman of Planning Commission has remarked, "it was the non-activism of the executive and the legislature that resulted in the activism of the judiciary which is the only forum for the citizen to seek legal remedy.

1. Ibid.

2. The Hindustan Time, Jan. 20, 1997.

A situation has now come where the judiciary has to intervene because of the failure of the other two organs of the Government."[1] However, the judiciary has not encroached either field; it has simply become more active to carry the duty issued by the constitution. Fortunately it has not shirked its duty. It is true to the constitutional obligation. Mr. Kuldip Singh, former Supreme Court Judge, has aptly observed, "It is just that the courts have become more watchful on the legislature and the executive which is a responsibility bestowed on it by the constitution"[2]. The legislators, of course, have gone wide off the mark and have kept themselves busy with petty selfish ends; likewise the executive has played foul even at the cost of national interest and no sense of accountability has shaken their conscience; it resulted in chaotic administration - utter failure in all walks of life. President Dr. Shankar Dayal Sharma in his address to the joint session of Parliament which began on 20th Feb. 1997, accepted the very fact, "In the past, our inability to come to grips with these challenges was responsible for our failure .....". (This sentence was deleted from the speech and there was much uproar in the house). Again, "Its aim would be to bring about greater transparency and accountability at all levels in the quest for an effective and responsive administration."[3]

1. The Hindustan Times, Feb. 10, 1997.
2. The Times of India, Feb. 18, 97, P. 9.
3. The Hindustan Times, Feb. 21. 1997.

In fact, maladministration has bred rampant corruption all over the country. People have lost faith in the legislature and the executive which ought to have worked sincerely and honestly for the welfare of the people. In such a dismal situation the judiciary came forward "to eradicate corruption which is permeating every nook and corner of the country", Justice M.Shamim observes, "the founding fathers of the constitution envisioned legislators as men of character, rectitude and moral uprightness whose sole object was to serve the public with dedication, to be open, truthful and legal."[1] Gone are the days when the legislators and the officials thought themselves to be public servants. Now the law makers violate the laws, spoil the oath taken at the time of holding office and forget to keep promises made in their manifesto; all is done for their petty gains and they never give thought to the sufferings of the people. If the judiciary has come forward to relieve people of their grievances, they have started frowning on it. Former judge of the Supreme Court, Mr. Kuldip Singh, is apt in his observation, "despite 50 years of independence, there was rampant corruption and violation of human and environmental laws. If the judiciary performs its role in a better, effective, enlightened and active manner, there is nothing wrong about it."[2]

It is matter of great satisfaction that unlike the other two organs of the Government the judiciary is discharging honestly its assigned duty despite many pulls and pressures.

1. The Times of India, April 13, 1997, p. 17.
2. The Hindustan Times, Feb. 19, 1997.

Its bold and enlightened verdicts in every field have led people to believe in the wisdom of the courts which are "eminently necessary and have a great meaning for preventing the executive and the legislature getting arbitrary and wayward".[1] At least we should be honest and bold enough to stand by the judiciary in the present circumstances instead of being dogs in the manger.

3. Methods of Judicial Review

The Indian constitution has provisions to empower Courts other than the Supreme Court or the High Court to issue writs if the Parliament makes a law. But no such law has yet been passed so only the supreme Court and the High Courts have power to issue such writs. The word writ (in Latin 'Breve') means a formal letter of a business character. A writ is a formal writing issued by authority of law and is employed for the purpose of acquiring jurisdiction of a person or his property or compelling him to appear in a court of law. There are five methods of judicial review.

i) Habeas Corpus*

The term Habeas Corpus literally means to 'have the body'.

1 The Hindustan Times, Jan. 15, 1997.

* Notable dissent of Hon'ble Justice Mr. H.R. Khanna in the case of Adm. (Jabalpur) vs. Shiva Kant Shukla in AIR 1976 Supreme Court. p. 1207, seems to have correctly summed up the various facts of the writ of Habeas Corpus.

Such writ is an order issued by the court upon a person who has detained another to produce the latter before the court in order to let the Court know on what ground he has been confined and to set him free if there is no legal justification for the detention. The use of this writ is to test the legality of the detention of a person. The writ may be addressed to any person whether an official or a private person who has another person in his custody and disobedience to the writ is met with punishment for contempt of court. The writ of Habeas Corpus is, thus, a very powerful safeguard to the subject against arbitrary acts not only of private individuals but also of the executive.

The writ of habeas corpus is available for the following different aims :

(a) The writ of habeas corpus is available to enforce the fundamental rights. Our constitution guarantees the right of personal liberty against the state by Art. 21 which says that "no person shall be deprived of his life or personal liberty except according to procedure established by law." If the authority of any law or in contravention of the procedure established by the law which authorises the detention or the imprisonment is itself invalid or unconstitutional, the High Court or the Supreme Court may issue a writ of habeas corpus against the authority which has kept the person in custody and order the release of the person under detention.

(b) It will also issue where the order of imprisonment or detention is *ultra vires* the statute which authorises the imprisonment or detention.

The writ of habeas corpus is, however, not issued in the following cases :

(i) Where the person against whom the writ is issued or the person who is detained, is not within the jurisdiction of the court.

(ii) To secure the release of a person who has been imprisoned by a court of law on a criminal charge.

(iii) To interfere with a proceeding for contempt by a court of record or by Parliament.

ii) Mandamus

The term Mandamus literally means "we command". In fact, it is an order which commands a person or body to do that which is his duty or its duty to do. The writ is issued in the name of the State to an inferior tribunal, a corporation, a board, or a person, commanding the performance of an act which the law specifically enjoins as a duty resulting from an office, trust or station. It is a discretionary remedy and the High Court may refuse to grant mandamus where there is a alternative remedy for redress of the injury complained of Regarding the enforcement of fundamental rights, the question of alternative remedy does not weigh so much with the court since it is the duty of the Supreme Court or the High Court to enforce them. In India, mandamus will lie not only against officers and other persons who are bound to do a public duty but also the Government itself since Arts. 226 and 361 provide that appropriate proceedings may be brought against the Government concerned.

The purpose for which a writ may be issued may be stated as under :

(i) The writ of mandamus may be issued to enforce fundamental rights. If a public officer or a Government does some act which violates the fundamental rights of a person, the court may issue a writ of mandamus.

(ii) The writ may be issued to enforce the performance of a statutory duty where a public officer has power conferred by the constitution or a statute.

(iii) The writ may compel any person to perform his public duty where it is imposed by the constitution or a statute or statutory instrument.

(iv) The writ may compel a court or judicial tribunal to exercise its jurisdiction when it refuses to exercise it.

(v) The writ may direct a public official or the Government not to enforce a law which is unconstitutional.

The writ of mandamus will not be granted against the following persons :

(i) The President, or the Governor of a State for the exercise and performance of the power and the duties of his office or for any act done or purporting to be done by him in the exercise and performance of those powers and duties, (Art. 361).

(ii) Mandamus may not be used against a private individual or body whether incorporated or not except where the state is in collusion with such private party, in the matter of contravention of any provision of the constitution or a statutory instrument.

iii) Prohibition

The term Prohibition literally means "to forbid". This writ is issued by the Supreme Court or a High Court to an inferior court to forbid the latter to continue a jurisdiction which is not legally vested in it. Actually it is issued to stop illegal jurisdiction. Prohibition is not available against a public officer who is vested with judicial function. In India a writ of prohibition may be issued not only in cases of absence or excess of jurisdiction but also in cases where the court or tribunal assumes jurisdiction under a law which itself contravenes some fundamental right.

iv) Certiorari

It literally means "to be certified". It has been defined as a prerogative writ issued from a superior court, directed to one of inferior jurisdiction, commanding the latter to certify and return to the former record in a particular case. This is a remedy also used in many jurisdictions, to review the procedure of inferior officers, board and tribunals in which case the administrative agency is considered as a lower tribunal exercising judicial functions. There are three requisites before the writ can be issued :

(i) There should be a tribunal or officer having legal authority to determine questions affecting rights of subjects and having a duty to act judicially.

(ii) Such tribunals or officers must have acted without jurisdiction or in excess of the legal authority vested in such quasi-judicial authority, or in contravention of the rules of natural justice.

(iii) The Supreme Court had taken a view that the writ of certiorari would not be issued against purely administrative action. The writ would be issued only if the authority has a duty to proceed judicially.

A tribunal may be said to act without jurisdiction in any of the following circumstances :

(i) Where the court is not properly constituted that is to say, where persons who are not qualified to set on the tribunal to hear the complaint.

(ii) Where the subject matter of enquiry is beyond the scope of the tribunal.

(iii) Where the court has taken jurisdiction on the basis of a wrong decision of the facts upon the existence of which the jurisdiction of the tribunal depends.

(iv) Where there has been a failure of justice either because the tribunal has violated the principles of natural justice or its decision has been obtained by fraud or collusion.

(v) When the decision of an inferior tribunal is vitiated by an error apparent on the face of the record'; it is liable to be quashed by certiorari.

v) Quo Warranto

It literally means "by what warrant". The writ quo warranto is issued to prevent illegal assumption of any public office or usurpation of any public office by any body.

(i) The office must be public and it must be created by a statute or by the constitution.

(ii) The office must be a substantive one and not merely the function or employment of a servant at the will and pleasure of another.

A writ of quo warranto may be refused where it is vexatious or where it would be futile in its result.

Thus, it is a very powerful instrument for safeguarding against the usurpation of public offices which are meant for public welfare.

To sum up the role of judicial review in a democratic system, it is not only theoretically relevant but also practically necessary. It helps democratic values grow luxuriantly. It is out to see if even an oridinary person is getting what falls to his due share. It has the capacity and the insight to meet changing circumstances. The task of the judiciary in the words of Justice Frankfurter (U.S.A.) is "to pierce the curtain of the future. Judges must be aware of the changing social tensions in every society which make it an organism, which demand new schemata of adaptation which will disrupt it, if it is rigidly confined."[1] No doubt the Indian judiciary is true to the words of Justice Frankfurter and intends faithfully to pave the way for the future.

1. The Hindustan Times, March 17, 97.

CHAPTER THREE

Colour and Culture of Present Politics

Before independence politics was the most powerful means to serve the country even at the cost of one's life. It was open to all that desired to sacrifice their lives on the altar of the country. People had experienced British administration to the full; they determined to end it though it was not an easy task. For the overthrow of the British rule a mass awakening and an indomitable will was necessary since people had been groaning under the yoke of slavery for a long time and had not imagined that they could raise their heads against injustice and cruelty. But tolerance had its own limits and India was mentally prepared to thwart what was alien to man and his progress. A galaxy of patriots came forward for this noble cause; politics was taken up as the means to serve the country. It was clear to all that there was no room for self-service. Irrespective of caste, colour or cult, the country was first and all other things came afterwards. Politics with this glorious purpose began to churn the blood of the people. People started feeling oneness among themselves. At this juncture persons of mighty actions like Gandhi appeared and defined politics as "applied religion" which was a dynamic force. This spiritualization of politics was essentially a progressive move towards justice and truth because any kind of oppression and exploitation was intolerable to an awakened soul. Thus politics was a mass movement for the liberation of all alike, the rich and the poor. It was comprehensive and all-embracing in scope and self-sacrificing in nature. It had deep moral and spiritual aspiration. It was a great cementing force for people of different mental make-up. It was a powerful defence against the impact of an alien political power in the country. In a nutshell politics was the religion of humanism.

After independence politics fell prey to ambitious persons and the values, which were the very foundation of the thinking of our politicians, began to wane. So, it began to fall on its evil days; it drifted away from well conceived goals. The concept of Swaraj was pushed behind and on the lines of the West things began to take shape on Indian soil. The parliament was invariably echoing with the sound of a new vision-a vision of social justice and equality, no struggle between haves and have-nots. It was, indeed, a pleasant dream. The innocent masses of the country had full faith in the wisdom of their parliamentarians who were (and are and will be too) the sole guide to decide the fate of the nation. Many catchy slogans were coined to make people believe they were heading towards a predestined goal. People went on believing and supporting them with unflinching faith in the hope of realising the dream of the freedom fighters. But all the time things went on worsening instead of improving. People hardly knew that most of their representatives had begun to think in terms of self and not of the country. They had an axe to grind even at the cost of the country. They forgot completely Gandhi's talisman, "Recall the face of the poorest and the weakest man whom you may have seen and ask yourself if the step you contemplate is going to be of any use to him. Will he gain anything by it? Will it restore him to a control over his own life and destiny? In other words will it lead to swaraj for the hungry and spiritually starving millions."

Our officials and representatives could neither see nor recall "the face of the poorest and the weakest man" and the long cherished vision turned into a mess. Even children had to spend their innocent childhood in earning bread and butter. Ironically enough, after a whole day's work they could not get a square meal. The common man lost all hope, dignity and grace in life which was expected and promised at the dawn of independence.

A careful study of the past fifty years brings out the factors which are responsible for this rapid fall of values in politics which has influenced even public life.

Factors Influencing Politics

i) Casteism and Communalism

A close peep down memory lane brings out the by-gone days when different castes made the thread of nationalism strong and lasting. During the struggle for freedom people of all castes, cults and sects stood against the British empire like one man. Their first priority was the service of the country since it was clear to them that their welfare lay in the emancipation of the country. Hence, their loyalties were meant for the country. But after independence these loyalties were divided into castes and communities. Post independence politics encouraged people to go in divergent directions. The picture of a new society free from the evils of casteism was receding. The casteism which had somewhat gone underground by the efforts of social reformers during the years of struggle, was revived with all its evil forces. Politics became a pot full of pores leaking ominous effects into society. It disrupted the entire sense of loyalty to merit; and all politicians who became the leaders or so called heralds of justice and equality over-night, brought off desired fruits and flourished luxuriantly at the cost of the sentiments of the nation. A healthy political culture which ought to have developed after the long struggle of ninety years (1857-1947) could not be conceived and all objective considerations were overshadowed by the evil of casteism.

Political parties have a lot to contribute to the revival of casteism just to capture power. They have always thought of casteism as a determinant in elections. They have made no hitch in choosing a candidate with reference to the caste composition of the electorate. The election strategy has as the only one brought all consideration to win the election. It has been reported on many occasions that the supporters of the particular candidate of a particular caste deprived people of franchise who belong to other caste and fake votes have been cast in their stead; the administration for some reason could do nothing to save the growing sapling of democracy However, the parties win the election quite fairly. They form the Government and rule over the country for five years. During their tenure the representatives are busy in building up a background for the next election rather than improving the condition of the people. Keeping in view the future election some political and administrative decisions are taken to please the people of a particular caste. This tendency has rapidly increased during the past fifty years. It has disappointed the non-partisan voter. It has intensified partisanship, sectional interests and to a great extent, has decided the fate of the candidate in the election. Undoubtedly, it has neutralized "the chances of cross-pressures". It is intolerable in the democratic system if persons having no caste background are denied opportunites in political, administrative and judicial fields. This tendency has proved to be disastrous for the system we have adopted hoping for equal share in power. It is a deliberate effort to go against the very basic tenets of democracy.

Communalism, the logical corollary to the above; has played havoc in Indian society. Modern thinkers and leaders like Gandhi, Nehru, Abdul Kalam Azad etc. have tried hard to efface the effect of communalism from Indian society even before independence but somehow this formidable task for a democratic society remained incomplete. The Indian National Congress and the Muslim League could not reconcile on any ground. As a result the dawn of independence witnessed a sensational bloodshed in communal riots in which "thousands of people were ruthlessly slain, hundreds were crippled and a large number of innocent children who did not know the meaning of communal riot or independence, became orphaned and starved to death. One incident at Calcutta shocked world history. "At dawn on 16 August, howling in a quasireligious fervour, Moslem mobs had come bursting from their slums, waving clubs, iron bars, shovels, any instrument capable of smashing in a human skull.... They savagely beat to a sodden pulp any Hindu in their path and stuffed their remains in the city's open gutters. The terrified police simply disappeared. Soon tall pillars of black smoke stretched up from a score of spots in the city, Hindu bazaars in full blaze."[1] Again — "Later, the Hindu mobs came storming out of their nighbourhoods looking for defenceless Muslims to slaughter. Never, in all its violent history had Calcutta known 24 hours as savage, as packed with human viciousness ..... By the time the slaughter was over, Calcutta belonged to the vultures. In filthy grey packs they scudded across the sky, tumbling down to gorge themselves on the bodies of the city's 6000 dead."[2]

The Great Calcutta killings still haunt the memory of the people even after 50 years of independence. People try to forget the galling experience of 1947 when the dying smoke assumes the holocaust either in the name of religion or community. Alas ! we do not take any lesson and for petty political gains we thrust our people into the mouth of ruin. All these events have created caste as well as community consciousness which hampers the healthy political culture and democratic traditions from growth. For this political leaders by and large, are to blame.

1 Collins, L & Lapierre, D; Freedom at Midnight; Vikas Publishing House Pvt. Ltd., New Delhi, 1976, p. 28.

2 Ibid; p. 29.

Now the matter has come to such a pass that political parties, in order to avoid accountability, have started blaming other parties as 'communal' especially BJP. Perhaps, the most unique scene has been witnessed in our parliament when all parties (certainly some regional parties) have combined as the U.F. to keep BJP out of power. What an irony it is ! that most of the parties which have economic and social ideology for a particular community, today claim to be secular and non-communal while they have virtually no ideology for the nation as a whole. It needs no further elaboration as the facts speak for themselves. Indeed, they are successful in their aim today but tomorrow the situation may be repeated with more evil effects. In future there may be any other 'Front' to keep other parties out of power branding that party 'Communal'. It is ironical that all the parties claiming to be secular and well wishers of the nation, are not in a position to form the Government.

ii) Religion and Language

India is called the land of religion and philosophy where a number of religions and cultures have flourished freely and people of different religions live together like members of a family. Religion has been very closely associated with politics. It has not only assuaged suffering humanity but also helped people to maintain law and order in society. Persons like Swami Dayanand, Swami Vivekanand, Gandhi and Tagore who grasped the spirit of religion in the true sense, have shown practically that both can go together hand in hand. Both are complimentary rather than contradictory to each other. People relied on this thesis and worked whole-heartedly for the liberation of the people. These thinkers have realized the creative force of religion; they have hardly approved creeds, cults and ceremonies as the guiding principle in life. Morality is the very basis of true religion. No sooner is morality lost than man ceases to be religious. Politics can not exist without religion as the latter is a great cementing force among people. In the words of Gandhi, "Politics bereft of religion are a death trap because they kill the soul." Hence, politics is unextricably woven with religion which means an energetic move towards justice and truth since a truly religious man cannot tolerate any sort of exploitation or oppression. As Dr. Radhakrishnan defines "politics but an applied religion," it inspires man to serve selflessly his fellow beings. Politics through religion provides man all that adds charm and dignity to life. This ideal was the very foundation of the Indian National Movement.

After 15 August, 1947, the long cherished ideal of the incorporation of religion in politics was pushed into oblivion as it hindered self-service. The statesmen and the politicians were busy in the heated debate as to whether politics and religion can go together; people were divided in their opinion and the politicians who are the sole guide of the country, have accepted the division of religion and politics. Neither had they time to think over the issue deeply nor could they heed Gandhi's sagacious words "To try to root out religion itself from society is a wild goose chase. And were such an attempt to succeed, it would mean the destruction of society". The politicians are the very members of this assorted society who live in and through a religious background, nay, their life is governed by religious apprehensions. Is it possible for these men to serve the country without religious fervour? If they try, it is hypocrisy or no service at all. To quote Machiavelli, "Wisdom consists in being able to distinguish among dangers and make a choice of the least harmful."

It cannot be gainsaid that English has played a vital role during the struggle for freedom but it is a fact that it has never become the language of the masses. After independence our leaders were confronted with the problem of language especially the national language. It was but natural and indispensable that they should have thought freely and fairly above all pride and prejudice of some Indian language. In the constituent Assembly a long debate was held and eventually consensus emerged in favour of Hindi not because "this language was rich in literature and others were not, but because this was spoken by the majority of people in the majority of regions and states." Hence, the architect of the constitution laid down in Article 343 that (i) Hindi in Devanagari script shall be the official language of the union; (ii) English shall continue to be used for all official purposes for which it was being used immediately before the commencement of the constitution and for 15 years after such commencement." The problem has remained unsolved. Many efforts have been made through various commissions to settle the linguistic question and principally Hindi has been accepted as the medium of mass communication. Later on the Kothari

Commission recommended the Three Language Formula in which regional languages were encouraged. Many times there was furore in the parliament over the question of Hindi and English but the Government did not make any effort to replace English by Hindi. But on 4 September, 1959 Prime Minister Nehru announced, that English "as an alternate language" would remain "as long as people require it".

During the past fifty years an elite class has emerged in our society which, due to its latent interests, does not like English to be replaced by Hindi. It has become a status symbol for them. Moreover, their vested interests do not allow them to put off the mantle of English. As a result most of the people suffer in the country and the Government remains unaware of the fact that common man is drifting away from the national current which is a sure sign of alienation. Whenever the few nationalists raise a hue and cry for the promotion of Hindi, other leaders create a feeling among people that Hindi is being imposed on non-Hindi people. They advocate strongly the use of English at the cost of Hindi. This feeling has done a great harm to national integration and solidarity. Dr. Radhakrishnan warned us long ago, "There was some hesitation in this matter when it was thought the study of Hindi was being imposed by the Government. We should see to it that such ideas do not prevail[1].

Our country is of a composite character. Its unity of purpose and vision has been expressed through many

1 Radhakrishnan's speeches & Writings : Publication Division: Series 11; p. 138.

languages. We must keep the fact in mind that the Indian heritage is contained in all languages, so none can be neglected. All languages have the soul of India. But it will be dangerous if the English language flourishes at the cost of the Indian languages due to the vested interests of a few. The politicians must avoid any effort to damage the thread of solidarity of the country by dividing people and their loyalties in the name of language.

If we are true to the soul of India and like to raise ourselves above linguistic rivalry, the fact remains undisputed that recently serials like Ramayana, Mahabharata, Chanakya, Sri Krishna, etc. have been fully enjoyed all over the country. It has proved that Hindi is the only language of mass media.

iii) Regionalism

Regionalism is also one of the most powerful factors which have influenced politics in India after independence. It has encouraged people's love and loyalty for a particular region in preference to the country and surprisingly enough in certain cases, in preference to the state of which it was a part. After independence it is seen all over the country. The feeling of regionalism in the hands of politicians whose sole aim is to grab power, has taken the form of "well conceived and well organised agitations and campaigns" which have certainly disturbed the harmonious tone of the country. Regionalism, in its romantic political colour, has sprung forth in four fold shapes : (i) demand of people for certain states secession from the Indian union, (ii) demand of people for separate statehood, (iii) demand for full fledged statehood, and (iv) inter-state disputes.

Secessionism in India : The curse of regionalism fell on Indian politics when a few states expressed their desire to secede from the Indian union in order to become an independent sovereign state. First of all the pernicious attempt was made on June 50, 1960 by Dravida Munnetra Kazhagam (DMK) and the Nam Tamil (We Tamil). They had a well organised joint compaign for the secession of Madras State from India. They wanted a separate sovereign state as Tamilnad. They were so aggressive in their demand that they burnt publicly the maps of India minus "Tamilnad". Later on, the DMK put forth its demand that the states of Madras, Andhra Pradesh, Kerala and Mysore should be seceded from the Indian Union in order to form an independent "Republic of Dravida Nad". Fortunately, the campaign could not get support of the people outside Madras. On April 9, 1961 many members of the DMK formed a new party known as Tamil National Party under the leadership of E.V.K. Sampath who was an M.P. He advocated an amendment in the constitution that India should become a highly decentralized federation of autonomous linguistic states, each of which would "have the right to secede." Pt. Nehru decried strongly the proposal and termed it the "Balkanization of India" and averred in no uncertain terms that the DMK demand for independent state was "manifestly outrageous". The sixteenth amendment in the constitution put down such secessionist forces.

The Sikh Community under the leadership of Master Tara Singh demanded an independent state even during the struggle for freedom. After independence the demand for a separate Sikh state became aggressive. He named the demanded state as 'Khalistan'which consisted of the Gurgaon district of Punjab and Patiala and the East Punjab States union. (PEPsu) During the 1950s and early 1960s the Sikhs of Punjab started an agitation for a Punjab Suba. The agitation often turned violent in which people had to face loss of life and property. At last the centre conceded to the demand but this could not satisfy the Sikh community and the followers of Sant Fateh Singh revived the ideology of a Sikh homeland. They declared that the true and the only goal of Sikh politics was to establish a "Socialist democratic Sikh homeland in north India." This feeling of separate state was intensified by Dr. Jagjit Singh, the general secretary when he set off for several countries to mobilise Sikh opinion in favour of 'Khalistan'. He resorted to militant activities to realize the dream of a Sikh homeland. Sant Fateh Singh did not approve of his militant activities since he considered them quite unfavourable and harmful for the Sikh faction. So, he expelled Dr.Jagjit Singh from the Akali Dal. During the 1980s the demand for Sikh land became more aggressive and extremism with all its fire and fury was seen all over Punjab. The golden temple became the main centre of these destructive forces. Extremism was at its peak and the centre was forced to take steps known as the 'Blue Star operation' due to which, later on, in 1984 the then Prime Minister Indira Gandhi fell to Sikh assassins' bullet. The whole country was shuddered.

Due to regional politics and secessionist forces the people of Punjab who have been, by nature, conscientious as well as gallant, have had to witness much bloodshed on the holy land of Guru Nanak.

The people of Mizo Hill districts of Assam put forth the demand for secession not only from Assam but also from the Indian Union. For this purpose they formed the Mizo National Front (MNF) and demanded, in strong words, an "independent Mizo state" consisting of the touching areas of East Pakistan and Burma. When the Government took to repressive measures, the Mizos organised armed agitation and started guerrilla warfare. They made a hue and cry to establish a Mizo State and intensified the feeling among people by fiery speeches and writings. The central authorities adopted all amicable measures to dissuade them but all in vain. They went on increasing militant activities due to which many people suffered and fell without any cause. The situation seemed uncontrollable so the centre had to deal with the rebels strongly and hundreds of them had to yield while others fled to save their lives but the secessionist forces could not be completely rooted out.

Again the Nagas of Assam raised their head under the leadership of Zapo Phizo who formed the Naga National Council for the fulfilment of the sinister purpose. In February 1950 Phizo conducted a plebiscite for an independent state for the Nagas and surprisingly enough 99 per cent of the Nagas favoured the demand. In the spring of 1955 the council created a great disorder and violence in the state. It posed a terrible threat to the centre so the army was called to deal with the rebels. In the army operation about 300 Nagas were killed and their area was declared a "disturbed area". The Indian army worked with patience and courage and was able to break up large rebel concentrations and to destroy their hideouts. The central authorities made frantic efforts for peace and harmony but the rebels did not give up their "hit and run" tactics.

Demands For Separate Statehood :

Reorganization of States : The problem of regionalism can also be seen in the form of the demand for separate statehood in many parts of the country. The makers of the constitution had abolished the then designations and classified states into three categories. Category A comprised Governor's Provinces as formerly known. These provinces included Assam, Bihar, Bombay, Madhya Pradesh, Madras, Orissa, Punjab, Uttar Pradesh and West Bengal. Category B included all Princely States, Hyderabad, Jammu and Kashmir, Mysore, Patiala and East Punjab States' union, Rajasthan, Saurashtra and Travancore-Cochin. Some of these were big Princely states while others were "formed by the merger of about 275 smaller Princely states". Chief Commissioner's Provinces fell into Category C which included Ajmer, Bhopal, Bilaspur, Coorg, Delhi, Himachal Pradesh, Kutch, Manipur, Tripura and Vindhya Pradesh. There were about 61 Princely States in it. Besides these three categories there were territories in Part D of the first schedule of the constitution. These were

Andaman and Nicobar islands.

Both category A and B had almost identical status. The category A was headed by a Governor while the latter by a Rajpramukh. Category C came under the direct control of the union Government Andaman and Nicobar islands were governed by the union Government in matters of the executive and legislature.

After independence leaders raised a voice for reorganizing states. So, in 1953 a commission was set up to look into the matter for an optimum solution. The commission was known as States Reorganization Commission (SRC). The SRC studied closely the situation in the status quo and arrived at the conclusion that the constitutcnt units of the Indian Union ought to be classified into two categories -

(a) "States" forming primary constituent units which have a constitutional relationship with the centre on a federal basis. Indeed, these units have a wide range all-over the country.

(b) "Territories" which could not be joined to any of the states due to their strategic or other considerations of vital importance. Therefore, they must be administered by the centre. The commission also suggested that the "Territories" might include the category C states and category D state territories. It was also proposed that these "terriroties" should be represented in parliament.

On the basis of the SRC recommendation in April 1956 the States Reorganization Bill was passed and the states were reorganised on a linguistic basis. The distinction which existed between category A and B was abolished. Category C was naturally ended. Some of these states were merged into the newly created states while others were re-designated as union territories. Here, the Government hoped that its sincere efforts to solve the problem must satisfy the people and undoubtedly the satisfaction was expressed to a great extent but the lust for power regional politics could not be satisfied. The apprehension of regional politics continued to loom in the parliament and the outcry of further reorganization of states deafened the ears of the countrymen.

Further Demand of Reorganization of States :

In spite of all sincerity and honesty of the Government the problem of the reorganization of states could not be solved for good but rather its linguistic foundation "made it more complicated". People deeply rooted in regional interest, desired a separate political entity and revived the agitation. They put the pressure on the Government for a further reorganization of states. The first forceful demand for a separate political entity was put forward by the people of the state of Bombay.

Bifurcation of Bombay :

According to the SRC recommendation Bombay

should remain a bilingual state - the Gujarathi speaking states and Marathi speaking districts should be incorporated in Bombay. These recommendations were adopted after a long controversy, besides the Marathi speaking districts of Madhya Pradesh were added to Bombay. The settlement, contrary to the expectation, resulted in bitter opposition. There were violent riots in Bombay and Ahmedabad; public life was disturbed and law and order was menaced. Many filthy and unruly incidents were reported. At last in August, 1969 Bombay was divided into two states. The division of Bombay gave a boost to regional politics in India which encouraged people in other states too.

Bifurcation of Punjab :

The bifurcation of Bombay started a chain reaction and the people of Punjab, under the leadership of the Akali Dal demanded a separate state for the Punjabi speaking people. The Hindus, too, grouped themselves under the leadership of Jan Sangh, Hindu Mahasabha and Arya Samaj and demanded a greater Punjab which included the union of Punjab, Himachal Pradesh, Patiala and East Punjab States. Both of the groups were determined in their demands and started campaigns and agitations which disturbed the peace and harmony of the country. The situation in Punjab became tense when Sant Fateh Singh, leader of the Akali Dal, gave an ultimatum to the Government that if his demand of a Punjabi speaking Suba was not accepted by 25 September, 1966, he would immolate himself. Considering the looming dangers over national integrity, the centre, on November, 1, 1966 got ready to divide

Punjab on a linguistic basis. The Punjabi speaking districts formed the state of Punjab and Hindi speaking districts formed the new state of Haryana and the Hindi speaking hilly areas of Punjab were transferred to Himachal Pradesh. Again regionalism came out victorious over national interests.

Reorganization of Assam :

Fired and inspired by the bifurcation of Bombay and Punjab, the people of Assam formed the All Party Hill Leaders Conference (APHLC) and demanded a separate hill state in clear cut words. There were long discussions and exchanges of hot words between the APHLC and the centre. There were violent agitations all over the state. The matter became grave and all activities for the development of the people came to a standstill. At last the Government agreed to organise Assam on a federal basis. The APHLC got ready on 18 January, 1967 to accept the arrangement of the Government but the Assam Pradesh Congress Committee not only disapproved the arrangement but also opposed it by saying that the hills and the plains of Assam were closely linked together and therefore neither of these can be overlooked. The matter came to a deadlock due to the rigid attitude of the APHLC and the demand for a separate hill state was revived again.

The Government had to yield to the demand for a separate hill state. In April 1969 Parliament passed a (22nd amendment) Bill and on 2 April 1970 a separate hill state known as Meghalya came into existence. This was an autonomous state within Assam. It was provided with its own legislature and council of members. But the monster of regional politics did not cease its function. On 30 September, 1970 the Meghalaya Assembly pressed the centre to convert the state into a full fledged state. At last, the demand was accepted in January 1972. The victory of regional politics encouraged other leaders of short stature who preferred regional interests without thinking about future repercussions. On the pattern of Shiv Sena, the Lachit Sena was formed in Assam which started a movement against the people who hailed from other states. They asked such non-Assamese to leave the state immediately. They threatened such persons especially the business class of their life. The movement created panic all over the state. The law and order was at stake. The movement became so intensified that the students under the leadership of the Lachit Sena called for a boycott of 26 January (Republic Day) celebrations. It was a clear threat and insult to the constitution of India. However, the situation was brought under control by the use of force but it did not mean the end of secessionist forces.

Briefly speaking, one success in regional politics has entailed other demands for separate states which intend to endanger national unity. Among such demands is the demand of Jharkhand state which has gained ground after much blood shed. In fact, the demand was virtually accepted in 1996 by the united Front Government under the leadership of Prime Minister Deve Gowda. It has shown clearly that the secessionist forces are at work in the country and the

Government has to yield at last before them. This tendency is quite alarming for the future of the country.

After Prime Minister H.D. Devegowda's assurances of Uttarkhand as a separate state on Aug. 15, 1996, All Bodo Students Union revived its demand for a separate state with zest and zeal. After a long wait, it had a dialogue with the Prime Minister but no solution came out of it; Then ABSU concluded that the centre heeded only to force. Eventually, a committee was formed on the Bodo movement. More than half a dozen organizations are included in it and it gave a memorandum to the Prime Minister. All these organizations are trying hard to pressurise the centre to form a separate state which is supposed to be on the Western Bank of the Brahamputra river.

There are six organizations of Bodoland which are highly active in Assam for a separate state. They are held responsible for most of the major incidents of violence in the state. They are well equipped with modern weapons and face army action. In January 1997 the Union Home Minister Indrajit Gupta had to appeal to the BLTE (Bodo Liberation Tiger Force) for cease fire. Fortunately the BLTE not only responded to the appeal but also appealed to its rival organization the NDFB (National Democratic Front of Bodoland) to stop 'nefarious' activities. These organizations believe in militant activities and have well trained hardcore militants for realizing their sinister purpose.

The main organizations are as under :

1. Bodoland Army :

Its former name was Bodo Security Force. Now it is an armed branch of the National Democratic Front. It launches destructive and sabotageous activities to attenuate the State Government It is a staunch supporter of an independent Bodo State.

2. Bodoland Statehood Movement Council :

It was formed just before the Assam Legislative election. Its chicf aim was to have an independent state within India. It tried its best to prepare a suitable atmosphere in the state for the aggressive demand for a separate state. But its defeat in the election reduced its stature and its dream lay in shambles.

3. People's Democratic Front :

It was organized in the beginning of the year 1986. It has superseded ABSU in politics. It is said to have its relation with the National Democratic Front. It has six MLAs who have extended their support to the Assam Gan Parishad (AGP) to form the Government.

4. Bodo Women's Justice Forum :

It is human rights organization under the leadership of Anjali Daimari. It is the most active organization working for a separate state.

5. Bodoland Liberation Tiger Force :

It is a well-equipped militant organization. The militant members of ABSU are included in it. It had taken responsibility for the explosions on 29 and 30 December 1996 which sent a wave of panic throughout the state. It supports strongly the activities of ABSU.

6. All Assam Students' Union :

This organization under the leadership of Mr. Upendra Nath Brahm raised the demand for a separate state. Now it is called 'the Father of Bodo' though after Brahm's death its influence has weakened.

Demands for Full-Fledged Statehood :

Regionalism has appeared in Indian politics in the form of the demand for a full-fledged statehood. The fourteenth amendement in the constitution empowered parliament to create local legislature for certain territories which included Himachal Pradesh, Manipur, Tripura, Pondicherry and Goa, Daman and Diu. The other territories like the Andaman and Nicobar islands, the Laccadive, Minicoy Amindive and Delhi which were excluded from the Bill, started campaigns against this unjust policy of the Government. The agitation and campaign took serious forms that were almost threatening. There was much hue and cry in Delhi but the union Government turned down the demand for a full-fledged state. But at last the Government had to surrender to the demand of the politicians and Delhi was made a full-fledged state. It added a new chapter in the victory of regional politics.

Inter-State Disputes

Another form of growing regionalism in Indian politics is the dispute between or among states. Such disputes have assumed so serious a shape that they have marred the harmonious tone of a heterogeneous society. The states have left behind the interests of the nationa to please the people of one particular region. These disputes are minor if we examine them on the national canvas but due to the narrow outlook and petty politics they have become monstrous. The dispute between Mysore and Maharashtra created history in regional politics. The dispute was borne with a Bill on March 1960 providing for the division of Bombay into a Marathi speaking state to be known as Bombay.

Punjab-Haryana Dispute over Chandigarh is well known in Indian politics. The dispute went to the extent of threatening national unity when in 1966 the then Chief Minister stated categorically that the state was not willing to "surrender even an inch of its territory to anyone." The statement created ill-will and bitterness among the people of the two states.

Several other disputes such as Vishal Haryana and dispute over river water (Narmada, Krishna and Cavery) have made people interested in regional gains instead of national achievements. The dispute between Maharashtra and Karnataka over Cavery water has gone to court. The issues which can be settled through mutual dialogues, are expected to be solved by the courts. It shows people's deep interest in regional matters rather than the country. Not to say certain politicans who believe in regional political activities, have made these disputes complicated so that they may come into the lime light. As a result, a lot of time and energy of the country which could have been better utilized, was consumed in waste.

All these factors have contributed a lot to the thinking of the people and especially those who are in power since they have made an easy way to the corridors of power through these fissures of politics. They overlooked people's welfare. They started influencing people by raising petty clinches to gain power. After coming to power, they kicked out all ideals and kicked up a fuss in the House for nothing. The common man who cast his vote expecting a better life, got frustrated and depressed. They felt cheated. Their requests and protests fell on deaf ears. The leaders as well as officials could not rise above petty partisan interest. The system is largely absent in providing welfare; issues of public importance cease to be central to politics. This sorry state of affairs made people hopeless and they knocked at the door of the judiciary which fortunately responded; but the high ups tried to dodge with the help of their officials who were sharing the fruits of power. The courts realized the seriousness of the situation and assumed the role of an activist to ensure that nobody is above the law. Certain jurists turned out to be amicus curiae to help the court in restoring justice to people. The court came up to the expectation of the people. The Indian judiciary has miles to go so it needs "men who have", says Justice M.M. Punchhi, "as three dismensions, personality — a good conciliator, good arbitrator and good mediator." However, the courts' aim, besides dispensation of law, is to ensure a life of amour propre.

CHAPTER FOUR

Criminalization of Politics

In post-emergency era during hearings in serveral cases the court found that the politicians were helped by criminals for the achievement of their aims in politics. Their main aim was to grab power at any cost; so money and muscle were their sole weapons. The court was convinced that the bureaucrats, too, helped their political bosses in this foul play. The criminals did their best during election; they captured booths and terrorised people to cast their votes in favour of a particular candidate. Truly speaking all types of tactics were used to win the election. When such cases were brought before the court, it did not hesitate to declare them void. The politicians were irritated at the judgement; their unhappiness was clear in their charges of court's role as judicial activist. The election commission has reported many cases of atrocious deeds during elections but due to lack of legal steps in this direction, the business of politicians, bureaucrats and criminals went on flourshing day by day. After Mrs. Gandhi's death, Indian politics got a new turn; it was more horrifying that the criminals started dominating politicians and they got their entry into the House. To the surprise of the court, the seasoned politicians who can not think of separating from power, have harboured the criminals. The court was alarmed at this new colour in Indian politics. Some amici curiae helped the court to unearth this unholy nexus which has damaged democratic institutions. The court is hearing such cases. It is expected that the guilty will not be spared.

(i) Politico-Mafia Nexus : It was an uphill task for any other wing of the Government to break off the politico-mafia nexus. It is the judiciary of India which has given a lethal blow to this undemocratic tie. The judicial activities besides in legal field, have awakened people to the ideals for which it stands. It is a great social service on the part of the Indian judiciary. Its step is to ensure rule of law; as Justice Verma has put it, "Preservation of democracy may be difficult if governance of country is not done by rule of law". Any attempt in any form if it flouts rule of law, will be frustrated by the guardians of the constitution. The Indian Judiciary is fully aware of its accountability to the constitutional ideals; in the present crisis it has determined to stand up to all those that do away with the rule of law which is the corner stone of democratic institutions. The new colour of politics which the executive and legislature seem to share, is quite alien to the spirit of a democratic system. The court is fully conscious of it; and its crucial role in shedding it, cannot be brushed aside. To quote Justice Verma again, "Time has come when judicial accountability for the judiciary cannot be ignored. While the judiciary must respect the other organs including their instrumentalities, its mandates ought to be honoured by others. Power must be used for the public good."

The horrible scene on Oct 21, 1997 in the U.P. Vidhan Sabha during the confidence motion, is proof of the fact that the House is activated by leadership based on tactics, not by democratic ideals. If such incidents are not checked in time by the legislature, it will be mandatory for the judiciary to step in to ensure rule of law. However, such energumens for power must be put down.

(ii) Criminal Culture : An alliance of politicians with criminals is the definition of politics in post-independent India; endemic corruption is their promising lad. It is purely a game of power which has to be won by hook or by crook. Politics has become a lucrative profession in which the most unfit persons of other professions can fare well. Self-effacement and moral fibre are no more prerequisites for a member of a political party. No training or calibre is required in today's politics. Above all no accountability to anyone. Here corruption is no longer immoral. It has become amoral. Indeed it is a bonanza. The politicians have a single motto—to enjoy the fruits of power. High political aspirations to be at the top in both power and wealth dominate political ideals. Politicians are ever distinguished persons. They always keep an aura around themselves. "A politician accused in several criminal cases, even as he continues to reside in a sprawling government bungalow, is ordered to be tried, not where millions of such accused are tried but in a special makeshift air-conditioned court ! Another of the species is not arrested until — and in fact not even immediately after — a court orders the arrest; instead, he is left alone to surrender in a court at a time of his choosing, and then is taken, not to prison but to a well-appointed guesthouse!"[1] Indeed, a privilege. Even in the prison they are in a role.

1 The Hindustan Times; Aug 22, 1997.

This play-acting is not accidental but a part of an elaborate game plan. The Hindustan Times (July 1, 97) comments on the arrest of Mr. Laloo Prasad Yadav, "And what a jail it has turned out to be ! The specially arranged air-conditioned room where he is lodged reportedly has all the facilities which would enable the 'prisoner' to function as if he were still a free individual". This is the species of today's politicians who have flourished and are flourishing unfettered.

Today, the politician-criminal nexus has become too strong to be easily broken. Even the administration is helpless against this knot. This nexus has given rise to all sorts of crooked means in politics. Even persons who are not trained in political affairs rise to power. Tricky cliches, power of money and muscle are their favourite weapons to win the election. "There was a time when criminalisation of politics meant the use of criminals and money power to achieve political ends. Today everything works the other way round. Criminals in politics use muscle power and money power to achieve their ends."[1] They have power uppermost in their minds. They are ruled by lust for power instead of reason. To them politics of goodness is the politics of the past. It has become outdated. Hence, feelings of sacrifice and self-denial are beyond their imagination. Violence is coupled with muscle and money power. It is the best weapon to survive in politics. It brings them the desired results. Violence, to them, is the solution to all problems. At first, violence was used to achieve political ends, but now it can be seen in every walk of life.

1. The Hindustan Times; Aug 31, 1997.

It is spreading fast and wide and preys on the public mind and is without a cure in sight. The different forms of violence are seen in the form of communal hatred, linguistic fanaticism, regional fealty, and caste and creed loyalty. All these are off-springs of violence in thought. They are gnawing at the vitals of the unity and integrity of the country. Surprisingly enough, the politicians exhort time and again that the people have to be in the forefront of the fight against "corruption, casteism and criminalisation of politics." People's welfare has been overlooked altogether; grand plans drawn for public good have met with complete failure. President K.R. Narayanan has regretted that "though we have registered significant successes, the fact of the matter is that we have not been able to abolish poverty, ignorance and diseases from among our people. The massive programmes that we have launched in these fields have not yielded the desired result." How ridiculous it is to talk of "the massive programmes" ! Successe is far from the imagination when the entire system has drifted into the hands of criminals who are left with scant respect for democratic norms and value based politics.

This criminal trend of politics soaked in violence, bathed in blood, stamped by racial discrimination, has thrown all values to the winds and divided people into sects of religion, caste, creed and sex. The criminals' entry into the House has shattered the very warp and woof of society. They have an easy access to the corridors of power. Due to them society has come to a sorry plight; people have a feeling of insecurity, fear and distrust. People believing in human values, are pushed off just for petty ends. All parties are to blame for this precarious situation. First, the political parties used criminals to achieve political ends, now the criminals have the upperhand in the party. They have occupied "high positions" in administration. The Prime Minister's chief secretary, N.N. Vohra, the convener of a three-member committee dealing with cases of criminalisation of politics, has gone into the allegations of such cases. His report points out that "a diabolical nexus between politicians, bureaucrats, some members of media and the judiciary and underworld dons was in existence." It has made one thing clear that the criminals cum politicians are able to influence every person to get things done. Their entry into the House is distressing and alarming as well. Recently the BSP-BJP which have combined to form the Government in U.P. to save the State from deteriorating law and order situation, have as reported in The Hindustan times (March 30, 97) "32 MLAs from different parties with criminal records, of these 15 are history sheeters and three have already been convicted. Samajwadi Party tops with 12 MLAs, of whom six are history sheeters. 8 BJP MLAs have criminal records, including three history-sheeters. BSP has six MLAs including four history-sheeters".

The number of criminals is on the increase in political parties. The problem will reach frightening proportions if it is allowed to go on unbridled. It will certainly make the entire democratic system a laughing stock. According to the election commissioner G.V.G. Krishnamurthy, as many as 700 of the 4,000-odd MLAs in the country are "history-sheeters", "a quaint euphemism which is probably used in India only to describe those with an unsavoury past. Forty MPs, too, belong to this unflattering category." Again, in the last Lok Sabha election, 1500 of the 13,952 contestants in nine states were "persons with criminal records. These persons have cases of murder, dacoity, rape, theft and extortion. Such entryism of the gangsters must be stopped as it is against democracy. The unholy nexus of political parties with the gangsters have put the electorates on the horns of a dilemma. It is really shocking that law-breakers become law-makers. During the session of Parliament, all the leaders of all political parties have told the nation about evils of corruption, criminalised politics, social disparities, hunger and illiteracy. I wonder if it needed a special session which cost Rs.7000 a minute. I would be happy if the leaders had pledged the nation not to give a ticket to a person of criminal record in the next election. The Hindustan Times aptly comments,[1] ".... but those with power vested in them to deal with it are either "helpless" or their actions are in the wrong direction. There are regional imbalances and absence of true federalism. But parliamentarians would invoke Article 356 at the drop of a hat, but would not care to dust up the Sarkaria report and implement remedial measures suggested there. They talk of the nexus between crime and politics but the Vohra report is doomed to be a subject for seminar discussions rather than a document for concerted national action." Indeed, this is dishonesty-sheer dishonesty. A foul play. A foul-up.

The nexus between crime and politics is flourshing luxuriantly day by day. It is fed on money and power in plenty.

1. The Hindustan Times; Aug. 27, 1997.

The so called law makers can go to any extent to save themselves from the clutches of law. They do their best for this purpose. If we have a bird's-eye view at the fodder scam in Bihar, we shall be taken aback to know their cheap but horrifying tactics. The CBI revealed to the Patna High Court that its officers were being threatened with death, as a result it was unable to arrest some top politicians. The courts found the CBI's fear true when the latter produced certain documents which clearly proved that the Central government was trying in every possible way to prevent the arrest of these top politicians. The CBI chief-officer Dr. U.N. Biswas further informed the court that 'in this situation the CBI could not be expected to arrest the accused persons even if it wanted to. He also produced in court a copy of a photograph showing many ministers and MLAs wielding spears and swords in front of the Raj Bhavan trying to chop off the head of his effigy with the district magistrate and superintendent of police of Patna standing nearby and doing nothing. The court expressed its deep displeasure over the attitude of the central Government for the delay in granting sanction for prosecuting some of the accused. The court further warned the Central Government counsel that it would expose all these persons, by name, who were trying to protect these politicians. Justice Jha's remark in this connection is worth quoting, "the sad reality we have to face is that it now seems established that the rule of equality is not being followed. He added that while the court could neither directly order the CBI to arrest any particular person nor change the obviously inflated and tainted reports being prepared by the intelligence agencies about the state, they were thinking seriously on these issues in order to prevent the entire system from collapsing."[1] One can see the fatal blow aimed at the entire system. By all odds the wicked nexus between crime and politics must be broken off for the survival of the system.

(iii) Role of Election Commissioner : Fortunately, the election commissioner broke the ice while all the party leaders were silent over the question of snapping off this tie between crime and politics. The three-member commission headed by Dr. M.S. Gill passed the order that "no convicted person will be allowed to contest elections even if an appeal against the conviction was pending in a higher court or the person was on bail." The commission's decision will apply to eight Assembly elections scheduled for the year of 1998. The decision is a bolt from the blue for all political parties. The decision has been taken in good faith of the country. It is a step to cleanse the system which is getting worse day by day. The commission's order is nota new one. Its aim is to strengthen section 8 of the Representation of the People Act (RPA), 1951 which provides that 'any convicted persons would stand disqualified from contesting elections to Parliament and state legislature for six years, people on bail and those who had appealed against such conviction were being allowed to contest.' Mr. Gill has written to the Govt. to 'recast and tighten' the section 8 of the RPA. In its directive the Chief Electoral Officers, the commission has observed, "the disqualification of candidature for elections under section 8 of the RPA, 1951 would commence from the date of

1 The Hindustan Times; July 2, 1997.

conviction, regardless of whether the person intending to be a candidate is put on bail or not (except, of course, the sitting MPs and MLAs who are covered under section 8 (4) of the Act.)

Section 8 (4) of the Act states that "none of the disqualification will take effect in case of a person who on date of convcition is a member of Parliament or a State Legislature, till three months have elapsed from the date or, if within that period an appeal or application is disposed of by the court." After reading the relevant RPA no one can blame the commission of working arbitraily. It has tried to enforce the Act. The commisison's step should be welcomed to save Parliament from the clutches of criminals. The RPA has already been supported by the judgements of three High Courts in which the courts have stated clearly that 'the suspension of sentence during the pendency of an appeal cannot be taken as "wiping out" the judgement itself.'

However, the commission's order has given rise to controversy. Some politicians who and legal experts have criticised the commission that it has gone out of its ambit to pass such order. They hold firmly that the Election Commission has no judicial power to bar people from contesting elections. In the opinion of Mr.R.K. Jain, a noted criminal lawyer, the commission's order "is not correct in law" as it violates Article 21 of the Constitution. It is the matter of the Supreme Court to interpret the meaning of conviction under the RPA. Even the High Courts are not unanimous on the issue. Some High Courts hold that conviction means final conviction after an appeal has been disposed of while the other courts hold the contrary position. On the other hand, some jurists have favoured the commission's decision. Mr. Kapil Sibal, President of Supreme Court Bar Association, is of the opinion that "conviction could only mean conviction by the trial court and there could not be a stay on conviction in law. Release on bail does not wipe off the disqualification under section 8 of the Representation of People Act since it is only the sentence that is stayed."

It is clear from the preceding discussion among the jurists that the commission's decision is a welcome move in bringing the issue of criminalisation of politics to the fore. If the move is an intervention in the work of the Government, it is in positive direction free from malice or prejudice. In fact, the commission has "reacted to the Executive's insensitivity to the problem". The Commission's intention cannot be put under a cloud. It has shot its bolt. It will help the electorates to keep the criminals out of legislature. The Government can help the commission by making an amendment in the Representation of People Act as comprehensive electoral reforms are urgently needed. But the real success of the commission's order depends on the political parties. The Hindustan Times (Aug. 30, 97) arrives at the right conclusion, "when parties rely on criminals to win elections, no amount of orders from the Election Commission can clean the system."

Surprisingly enough, our constitution does not speak a word about political financing which has posed a threat before the nation. The election laws are fully aware of the danger of black money entering the political parties day by day. Section 77 of the RPA puts restraints on election expenditure but the law has no provision "to regulate the flow of unaccounted funds into coffers of political parties." Hence financial corruption goes on without much challenge. In the beginning the political parties got financial aid from industrialists and big businessmen. By and by money began to play a vital role to win the elections; the politicians with allies started looking for new sources of money. At last, they got sources-kickbacks, commissions, kidnappings etc. Money began to flow to the political parties through foreign transactions. Hawala case in which top politicians are involved, drew the attention of the country to the problem of black money. This money was used to win the favour of one party or another. It also entered the Parliament. The JMM scandal in which former Prime Minister Narsimha Rao allegdly greased the palms of four JMM MPs, is a unique instance in India's history. The scandal has shown the power of money. It was a fraud, with the people of the country. It was a heinous crime on the part of both those who bribed and those who were bribed. The public servants whom people wanted topull down, held high positions quite brazenly for the full term. There is hardly any such example in democratic countries of the world. The Delhi High Court held former Prime Minister P.V. Narasimha Rao and 18 others guilty of criminal conspiracy and corruption and stated in its judgement, "He (Mr. Rao) with a view to save the Government headed by him, is prima facie a party to a conspiracy to bribe MPs and thereby win over their support. He was also party to the actual bribing of the MPs. It is not the job of the Prime Minister to hatch or be a party to such criminal conspiracy. Power intoxicates the best hearts as wine the strongest heads but then nobody can thrive on corruption. It is the froth on water, an inch deep and then mud. A Prime Minister must not sustain his power and position on the crutches of corruption ...... All ambitions including the ambition to remain perenially in power, are lawful except those which climb upward by means unlawful."[1]

1 The Hindustan Times; Sept 13, 1997.

CHAPTER FIVE

Corruption In Pulic Life

The Indian Judiciary has discharged the duty plainly laid upon it by the constitution without fear or favour. Whenever the laws were passed against the spirit of the constitution and challenged, the Supreme Court had stepped in fearlessly and declared them void. By exercising this power, the Apex Court has shown that it is the true guardian of people's rights and is constantly vigilant. The Indian Supreme Court between 1950 and 1975 "held more than one hundred union and state laws, in whole or in part, to be unconstitutional" under the power of judicial review. It was a hard blow for the legislators who tried to go by the board in regard to the sovereign will. The court frustrated their ill-will. Democracy was saved. During Emergency in 1975 Indian life was badly affected and the headway towards a welfare state came to a stand still. Hence, the Judiciary, too. "The rule of law was suspended, as anyone who opposed Mrs.Gandhi became a target for the police. This resulted in a spate of petitions in the High Courts, habeas corpus cases. The Government of India argued that Article 21, guaranteeing the Right to Life, had been suspended for the duration of the emergency. Therefore, the courts could not look into the petitions. Seven high courts refused to accept the argument, three high courts did."[1]

1 An article by T.V.R. Shenoy; The Hindustan Times; 29 Sept, 1996.

Thus, sensu stricto the judiciary failed to act. The executive was put in the shade. Consequently, both the politicians and the bureaucrats indulged in foul play. Foul-up prevailed everywhere. Even after the dark days of Emergency corrupt practices continued unchallenged and the situation in all walks of life kept on worsening. As the Supreme Court came to know about the violation of human rights and fundamental rights, it resumed the role of an activist with a vengeance. It gave a series of decisions defending people's rights. These decisions were hailed by the people but severely criticised by a lobby of politicians and bureaucrats. As time rolled by the nexus between politics and bureaucracy became strong; as a result many scandals were buried and surprisingly responsible persons buried their head in the sand. Defaulters were on the safe side. Scams and scandals went on multiplying which adversely affected public life; people were baffled at the discovery of the unthinkable dark deeds of the politicians and their accomplices. To quote Justice A.M. Ahmadi, "But, in recent years, as the incumbents of Parliament have become less representative of the will of the people, there has been a growing sense of frustration with the democratic process. The oridinary citizen has reacted in either o f the two ways. One group — whose members constitute a large majority of the population — has chosen to look upon these developments as an unavoidable feature of their lives and has adapted itself to these uncertainties while continuing to bemoan its destiny. The other group — which constitutes a very small minority — has chosen a more positive and innovative approach and has sought to achieve its objectives through the Judiciary."[1]

1 Quoted in the article by Bindheswar Pathak The Hindustan Times; April 28, 1996.

The daredevils of the latter group brought the scandals before the court through PIL. The court responded to their call and unhesitatingly brought many high-ups to the dock. Let us have a brief look at the corrupt practices which had started with the golden dawn of independence.

After independence, talking about value-based politics which once inspired people to join it for a noble cause, was just a prattle since Gandhi who was "necessary both to the Congress and the British while freedom had seemed far away, was to be relegated to the background."[1] At the very threshold of independence, Gandhi, "the saint with his phalanx of illiterate peasants could be put aside."[2] Now the Indian leaders who were thought to have better vision of freedom than the man of moral force came to the fore since "it was now the time for civilized negotiation between men who spoke the same unapocalyptic language."[3] These leaders with their new vision became the guide of the nation; in the name of service they began to enjoy power and pelf to such an extent that their kith and kin had privilege over the masses. The Congress leaders, in the words of Mr.Narayan, "at various levels had become a different breed altogether. Insensitive. Selfish. Calculating. Cowardly. Inept. Uncaring. Irresponsible. Greedy. Ease-loving. Opportunistic. Unprincipled and unashamed seekers after office and power and money."[4]

1 Edward Michael; The Last Years of British India; The New English Library, London 1967; p. 103.

2 Ibid

3 Ibid

4 Narayan S.D. They Betrayed You, Dear Mother; Vol I; p. 89.

Of course, they were soon found engaged in malpractices which resulted in maladinistration and dishonesty to the pledge they made at mid-night August 14-15, 1947.

In 1948 when Gandhi was told of a case of bribery by a minister's son by Manu (Minister's name was not disclosed) his face became red in anger. He was ready to talk to Nehru about it but the next day he was shot dead. The country had hardly forgotten the pangs of "massive migration, communal massacre, loot, rape and arson—scenes the like of which no eye had seen, no heart conceived, no human tongue could adequately tell"[1] than our leaders shocked the people by their disgusting demeanour. Amazingly, the persons who suffered for freedom, blamed the British Government for the sad plight of the people and promised Swaraj, overlooked the eerie things. People country-wide were much surprised at the discovery of malpractices in which many high-ups were involved.

I. Scams and Scandals in Public Offices

1. The Jeep Scandal

In 1948 the jeep scandal came to light in which the renowned scholar Mr. V.K. Krishna Menon was charged of taking kickbacks. At that time he was High Commissioner in Great Britain. After the invasion of India by Pakistan the Indian army which was poorly equipped to face any internal or

1 Krishna Iyer V.R. The Hindustan Times; June 28, 1998.

external threat, needed about 4603 jeeps. When Mr.Menon came to know it, he informed the Government of India in a telegram that there were about 1500 jeeps in quite good condition which can be purchased immediately. One jeep cost 3000 pounds. On the assurance of a profitabl deal the Defence Ministry sent an order for the purchase of the jeeps. The Department had to pay 65% of the amount in advance to the agency-Ante Mistances. Nine Months had passed but to the surprise of the Minister, not even a single jeep was sent to India. There was a long correspondence between the Ministry and Mr.Menon but of no avail. The Defence Ministry raised a hue and cry. Later on, after much embarrassment, in 1949 155 jeeps arrived at Madras harbour. These jeeps were in such a bad condition that they needed to be repaired even to reach the border. All these were fourth grade jeeps. Hence, good-for-nothing. When the matter was raised in the Parliament the order was cancelled. On enquiry the agency was found nowhere in England.

Afterwards Mr.Menon looked for another firm named S.C.K. Agency which made a solemn promise to send between 12-68 jeeps every month. But it also failed in its promise and could send only 49 jeeps in two years.

Likewise Mr.Menon had talks with J.C. Kenat & Co. for the purchase of rifles. The total deal cost Rs.3 crores and the company had to send the rifles within three months. The Defence Ministry was surprised when it did not receive even a single rifle after three months. So, the Defence

Ministry decided to cancel the order but Mr. Menon suggested that steel plates should be purchased in place of the rifles. Therefore, complying with Mr.Menon's suggestion the order for the same was placed. Again the same thing happened; six months passed but no steel plate was sent. So, the Government of India had to cancel the order. After an enquiry it was known that a person named Peter was behind all these firms. It was argued that most probably Mr.Menon himself did not know much about this man.

But, there was much furore in Parliament and an enquiry was demanded so that the truth might come to light. A committee was set up under the chairmanship of Mr.Anant Shayanam Ayangar to probe into the matter. After the enquiry Mr.Menon was found guilty and he too, admitted it with regrets. He was not taken to task; but on 30 September 1955, the then Home Minister Govinda Vallabh Pant informed the Parliament that the jeep scandal was closed. If any member was not satisfied, he should raise the issue during the general election. It was more distressing and surprising as well that Prime Minister Pt. Nehru inducted him into his cabinet as the Defence Minister instead of chastisement.

In spite of its commitment to do 'complete justice', the Indian judiciary had to remain a silent spectator since no member of Parliament or pro bono publico had taken the matter to the court. The Indian leadership, perhaps, did not think it right to go to the court for such petty matters.

2. *The Sirajuddin Diary Scandal*

Like today's Jain Diary in Hawala Scandal, in 1956 during an income tax raid on the house of Mohd. Sirajuddin some letters and diaries were found in which he had mentioned the names of those politicians whom he had given money to serve his purpose. Due to some reason or the other the scandal could not draw people's attention and it was buried deep. But seven years later some newspapers in Calcutta began to publish remarks about these diaries. Now people were alarmed and took the matter seriously. Mr. Surendra Nath Diwedi raised the matter in the Parliament and demanded an enquiry into the scandal to make things clear. After a long and hot discussion and unruly uproar in the Parliament, the then Petroleum Minister Mr. Keshav Deo Malviya confessed that he had taken kickbacks - Rs.10,000/-. Prime Minister Nehru set up a commission under Justice S.K. Das — a judge of the Supreme Court. Justice Das did his job conscientiously day in and day out. He submitted his report to the Prime Minister but the report was not tabled in the Parliament but Mr.Keshav Deo Malviya had to resign. Mr. Sirajuddin never felt nervous or discouraged during the enquiry but to the contrary, due to his strong hold in politics he got the favour of the politicians; not only this but also became their chosen one and got the contract of O.N.G.C. from Czechoslavakia. Favouritism prevailed.

Justice Das toiled in preparing the report on the basis of the facts; there was enough proof for the guardian of the constitution to bring the defaulters to book but no one bothered to bring the matter before the court to be decided according to the law of the land.

3. *The Mundhara Scandal*

In 1957 the Indian Parliament witnessed an unruly scene over an LIC Investment of Rs.3 Crore in the Mundhra shares. The congress stalwarts including Pt.Nehru's son-in-law Mr.Feroz Gandhi who was an M.P. put pressure on Pt. Nehru for the proper investigation into the case. At last Pt. Nehru had to yield to the pressure of the august House and a committee was set up under the chairmanship of Justice Mohd. Karim Chagla who was the Chief Justice of the Bombay High Court. Justice Chagla did his best in collecting all possible proof to do justice. In his report which was based on facts and figures, Justice Chagla brought the then Finance Minister T.T. Krishnamachari, the Finance Secretary Mr.H.M. Patel and the Chairman of L.I.C. in guilty. Mr Mundhra was charged of bungling Rs.160 crores. Apart from this, there were 180 charges against him. Justice Chagla stated categorically that the Finance Minister must own responsibility instead of passing the buck to his secretary. Pt. Nehru had to face severe criticism in the Parliament. Under pressure of the House Pt. Nehru had to remove him from the Finance Ministry but at the same time he was made a minister without portfolio. After some time as the matter cooled down Pt. Nehru made him the Defence Minister and in 1963 he was again made the Finance Minister. Indeed, favour out Justice Chagla scrutinised the case carefully and found many responsible persons guilty of misusing the power which was meant for public good. It was a strong tie between political bosses and bureaucrats who had an axe to grind at the people's cost. The Indian Judiciary was honest enough to bring the defaulters to task but it felt helpless for want of our vigilance and seriousness in the matters of national significance.

4. The Kairon Case

In 1964 the Punjab Chief Minister was charged of amassing wealth indiscriminately during his tenure. Mr. Kairon was said to have been a favourite of Nehru. The chief charges against him were about the establishments which were owned by either Mr.Kairon himself or his kith and kin. These were mainly Amritsar Cooperative Cold Storage Ltd., Kairon Brick Film Society, Prakash Cinema, Ludhiana Cooperative Cold storage, A light Cinema, Hissar, Nandan Cinema, Punjab Cold Storage Mukut House, National Motors, Amritsar; Neelam Cinema, Chandigarh, Capital Cinema Patiala and Neelam Cinema Faridabad.[1]

The Central Government set up an enquiry committee under the chairmanship of the former Supreme Court judge Justice S.R.Das, who looked into the charges against the Chief Minister Kairon. After an enquiry the report was submitted and Mr.Kairon was acquitted of many charges. But it was clearly mentioned that it was not practically feasible for the Chief Minister to keep an eye on each relative but it was also not proper on his part, being a highly responsible

1 Raj Kishore ed. Bhrastachar Ko Chunoti; Vani Prakashan, New Delhi 1995; p. 42.

person that he should overlook them altogether; they must be reckoned with. Therefore, he could not be held less responsible in this matter. There were many grave irregularities in various administrative matters for which none but he was responsible. At last after much hue and cry he had to step down from his post. All his kith and kin who had taken undue advantage of his position and abused his power, went scot free.

5. *The Nagarwala Episode*

The Nagarwala Episode was unique of its kind in the year of 1971. On 24 May 1971 at 11.30 am. Ved Prakash Malhotra who was the chief cashier in a branch of State Bank of India, New Delhi, received a call which directed him to handover Rs.60 lakh to the person who would speak a particular code as money was needed in doing some secret job in Bangladesh. He would get its receipt from the Prime Minister's office. The voices at phone were of Mr.P.N. Huxar and Mrs. Indira Gandhi as per Mr.Malhotra's version. Mr. Malhotra put the money in a brief case and reached the mentioned place on the Patel road. He handed over the brief case to the person sitting in a taxi after he had spoken the particular code. When Mr.Malhotra contacted Mr.P.N. Huxar for the receipt in the P.M. office, he was shattered when he found out that it was neither Mr.P.N. Huxar nor Mrs. Indira Gandhi who had rung him up. A shrill cry escaped his lips, "I am undone! I am robbed!"

Afterwards, it was known that it was Rustam Soharab

Nagarwala who had received the money from Mr. Malhotra. He was arrested and the sum of 30 thousand rupees was recovered from him. The court sentenced him to rigorous imprisonment. But he passed away under mysterious circumstances. In the Parliament the opposition party raised the question of the fake voice on the phone. The members of the opposition argued that Mr.Nagarwala had suffered from a paralytic attack on his face so it was not possible for him to produce the voice of Mrs.Gandhi. However, the matter was carelessly brushed aside instead of being taken seriously.

But, the Janta Party Government set up a commission. Justice P.Jag Mohan Reddy was its chairman. The commission worked hard but arrived at no logical conclusion. Even then it maintained that the working style of the P.M. Office in disposing of the matter was far beyond satisfaction; and certain things which were confessed by Mr.Nagarwala proved that there was something black in the bottom. It was some big conspiracy which was hatched by some highly stationed persons; Mr. Nagarwala alone could not have done it. Mr. Nagarwala's mysterious death mystified the case more.

6. The Karunanidhi Episode

In 1972 Mr. M.G. Ramchandran and Mr. M. Kalyan Sundram of the Communist Party along with other legislators and again in 1975 Mr. K. Manoharan and Mr.G. Vishva Nathan lodged a complaint to the President that the Chief Minister M. Karuna Nidhi, his fellow ministers and other office bearers of Dravid Munnetra Kadgam not only misused their power but also committed many acts of curruption and treachery. Due to persistent complaints a commission under the chairmanship of Justice R.S. Sarkaria was set up for proper enquiry into the matter. During the enquiry Mr. Karunanidhi and his colleagues were proved guilty in many cases such as bungling of rupees in crores and giving illegal licence to the industrialists. One of the cases which shocked the people country-wide was the purchase of tractors from Fergusoan Co. by the British company. Wallace Carter Wright and ploughing the fields of Mr. Karunanidhi. How the tractors reached India and who paid for them was a mystery. On the same lines another case was of Nathan Publication which in 1967 began to thrive as the Drumak came into power. The case brought out a number of malpractices at all levels of the Government including theft of income tax to the allocation of quota. Mr. Anil Dharmalingam, the Agriculture Minister at that time, with was charged bungling crores of rupees. He gave a contract to the Agency known as Pani Agency to sprinkle medicine from the air over the crops. In this contract there was a fake partner named Mrs. N.D. MahaLuxumi who along with Mr. Dharmlingam and Agriculture Director was to receive 66% amount out of the total payment to be paid to the Agency. The payment was made on July 14, 1970 and Mr. Dharmlingam received Rs. 20,000/- in cash. In this case Mr. Karunannidhi got Rs. 25,000/- by his secretary.

Again, both the Chief Minister and the Agriculture Minister were found guilty of taking 3 lakh 87 thousand, 7 hundred and 46 rupees on different occasions from different companies. Besides, Mr. Karunanidhi was also allegedly accused of amassing wealth beyond known sources either in his own name or his relatives. Many cases of buying property either by his son, nephew or secretary came to light. All these cases fetched him Rs. 15,21,276/-. The commission probed into 28 cases. Mr. Karunanidhi had direct or indirect involvement in all the cases. He could reap huge benefit from his power and position. No action was taken against him or his colleagues.

7. *The Deoraj urs Episode*

When in 1975 emergency was imposed on the country, Mr. Deoraj urs was the Chief Minister of Karnatak State. He thrived by misusing his power and position. His colleagues also did not lag behind in all sorts of corrupt practices. There were 25 charges against the Chief Minister. These charges were of abuse of power, corruption, malpractice, nepotism, partiality etc. On enquiry he was brought in guilty in some cases while in others his colleagues had direct involvement. People were shocked to learn that no action was taken against any of them.

8. *Malpractices During Emergency - 1975*

During the dark days of emergency people had witnessed all sorts of atrocities. Even the veteran leaders of the country were humiliated and put behind bars without rhyme or reason. The Government and its officials violated the law of the land; but they used the law according to their convenience and indulged in all sorts of irregularities. Moral or lawful standards in public life were thrown to the winds. After Emergency the Janta Party came into power. It set up a commission under the chairmanship of Justice J.C. Shah. It probed into the atrocities, malpractices, lawlessness during the period of emergency. During enquiry some eye-opening cases of corruption and lawlessness came into light.

(i) Misuse of Media : During Emergency the entire media had become a puppet in the hands of the politicians. It was completely at their disposal. They used it for their personal and selfish petty benefits; public interest was neglected altogether. The translators of Doordarshan and D.A.V.P. translated the congress manifesto. The artists of D.A.V.P. made designs of the election posters of Mr. Vidya Charan Shukla. The Department of Information and Broadcasting reprimanded the famous singer—Kishore Kumar. Thus, democratic institutions were used for purpose of the individual.

(ii) Financial Bungling : Search in Baroda Rayon, and Bajaj Group Co; special direction for Maruti Ltd.; import of an aeroplane by Dheerendra Brahamchari for his ashram, Mr. K.R. Puri's appointment as Governor of Indian Reserve Bank, T.R. Vardachari, T.R. Tuli, J.T. Satarwala, Air Marshal H.C. Diwan, as the Presidents of Indian State Bank, Punjab National Bank, Indian Tourist Development Corporation, and Indian International Aviation Corporation respectively are such cases in which all rules and regulations were put aside; and politicians in power and officials did what they pleased. Persons like Mr. Sanjay Gandhi who had no post in the

Government could call for explanations from any minister he liked. The Shah commission put a question on the emergency itself as its proclamation was not the question and held Mrs.Indira Gandhi responsible for it. Later on Mrs. Indira Gandhi was arrested. Unfortunately, the move of the Janata Government did not seem to eradicate corruption from public life; it was a case of revenge pure and simple. The leaders of the different parties could not stand united; they fell from their aim. And they fell foul of one another instead of falling into place. As a result the defaulters escaped and Mrs. Indira Gandhi came into power again. She took all the cases back. In this way all blackguards with all their black-deeds were men with a past?

8. The Maruti Car

The Government of India set up two committees in 1959 and 1960 to manufacture cars at a low price. But, due to the shortage of foreign currency, no plan could bear fruit in this field. In 1968 Mr. Sanjay Gandhi desired permission to set up a company for manufacturing cars at Gurgaon. Earlier the Government wanted to prefer public sector but Mr. Gandhi's proposal was given top priority in the private sector. Hardly had he applied for the industrial licence when the planning commission inspected his planning report and the then Chief Minister of Haryana Mr. Bansilal started taking special interest in it. Having put all rules and regulations aside, he allotted Mr. Gandhi 300 acres of land.

The Janta Government set up a commission headed

by Mr. A.C. Gupta to probe into the activities of Maruti. The commission collected all the facts and figures and submitted its report to the Government. It was said in the report that there was hardly any department of the Government which had not flouted all the rules and regulations to help the Maruti Industry. It further added that such a downfall in loyalty to the public sector was never seen before, all the lawful requirements were overlooked and all social and traditional customs and conventions were forgotten altogether. The Maruti shares were distributed to those who did not have any knowledge in this field. In February 1977 a handsome payment was made on fake names. At last, the Government nationalised the Maruti Ltd. The report of the commission was shelved and its all recommendations remained unheeded.

9. *The Oil Scandal*

The famous oil scandal took place in the year 1980. The Indian Oil Corporation issued a tender to purchase 3 lakh tonnes of purified oil and 5 lakh tonnes high speed diesel. Mr. Harish Jain who had easy and direct access to Mr. Sanjay Gandhi, got the tender. There was a bungling of 9 crore rupees in this purchase. An enquiry was set up but all the files related to the matter were found missing from the Prime Minister's office. The then Petroleum Minister Mr. P.C. Sethi had to resign but later on he was made minister again. Due to their strongholds in power both politicians and their accomplices went on flourishing on public money with no care for the law of the land.

10. The Antulay Case

The Antulay Case in 1982 flashed in the headlines of the newspapers due to which Mr.Antulay had to step down from the Chief Ministership of Maharashtra. In this case the active role of the press was applauded all over the country. Mr. Antulay collected funds in the name of Indira Gandhi Pratisthan and Trusts. It goes without saying that all these trusts belonged to the public sector but in fact they were used for personal ends. Those who invested money in these trusts, could get a quota of cement. If any industrialist donated money to either of the trusts, he was supposed to be free from all rules and regulations in his business. Hence, bonanza to them. Seeing the malpractices increasing day by day some daring persons like Mr.Ramdas Nayak, Mr. P.B. Samant, Mr. Mrinal Gaud and Mr. Kamal Desai field cases in different courts. It was, perhaps, the first example of awareness among people when they approached the court for a public cause. On 12 January 1982 Justice B. Lentin, Bombay High Court, held Mr. Antulay guilty. As a result, he had to resign from his post.

11. The Churhat Lottery Case

The Churhat Children's Welfare Society at Churhat, a town in Madhya Pradesh. The basic aim of this society was to work for the welfare of children, helpless and poor women and the propagation of health facilities in the state. The society began to conduct a lottery system for economic gains. In this lottery system administrative machinery was misused;

as a result, corrupt practices were prevalent in the economic field. People who were involved in the lottery system, were often charged of amassing wealth of 4 crores and 10 lakh rupees. Mr. Arjun Singh was the Chief Minister of the State of Churhat which was his hometown. People levelled allegations against the son of the Chief Minister Mr. Ajay Singh and his relatives as well. People raised a hue and cry all over the country; as they were becoming aware of growing corruption in the political arena. At last Mr. Arjun Singh had to quit his post. A commission was set up under the chairmanship of Justice Ramlingam but due to the untimely demise of Justice Ramlingam the enquiry could not be carried on further. The Government did not show any indication to punish the offenders.

12. The Bofors Deal

The Bofors Deal has been a much talked about case which involved even the name of the then Prime Minister Mr. Rajiv Gandhi and other top politicians of the country. The ruling party had to face much criticism but the people all over the country became eager to know the names of the persons who received kickbacks in this deal. Mr. V.P. Singh who was the Finance Minister at that time left the party on this issue. He promised the Indian people to unearth the case in order to bring the culprit to book. He made corruption the main issue during his election campaign. He said that he would let the people know the truth about the Bofors deal if he won the election. At last, he became the Prime Minister of the country; and there was a wave of joy among the people as they were sure that the cat of the Bofors case would come out of its bag. But for known or unknown reasons he was out in the cold in this matter and things remained unchanged.

In 1986 the Indian Government had a contract with the Swedish Company to purchase 155 guns. In this contract a kickback of Rs. 65 crore was given to different persons as commission but even after much outcry the names of the commissioned persons could not be disclosed. The Defence Minister had to resign. However, the case was referred to the CBI which made meticulous efforts to get the names of the beneficiaries. The CBI had to clear out the obstacles of the Swedish laws. During the tenure of Mr.Rao's Government no progress was made in the case. But people continued their demand of disclosing the offenders' names. When Mr. Deve Gowda came into power, people put pressure on him. The Government really, did a commendable job in this case and the CBI succeeded in getting the papers of the Bofors case through the Swedish Court. The country heaved a sigh of relief. A few names have been disclosed while others are yet to be known to the people. But the task does not end with the disclosure of the names. People are waiting to see if the offenders get their punishment or not.

It is crystal clear from the above discussion that both the Executive and the Legislature have failed on various fronts to act as responsible wings of the Government; and with the passage of time things have become worse than before. The Apex Court from its inception in 1950, has played a role of a traditional court adjudicating cases of constitutional importance such as Zamindari Abolition or abolition of Privy Purses etc. And the then leadership had exhibited remarkable patience in bearing with such riff-raffs who hit the democratic system as hard as they could. Also it is amazing that no parliamentarian, no man of law and no public body or organisation approached the court to put a restraint on these underhand tactics in public life. Even those who were in the position of putting them down, pulled their punches and the defaulters never saw the day of reckoning. But what stands unchanged, unaffected till today is people's unflinching faith in the judiciary. Every time a judge either from the High court or the supreme court was called upon for a fair and free probe and the judge with all probity and judiciousness, did his job and never saw eye to eye with bizarre things. He did not blank out the facts whether they were related to the high-ups or an ordinary citizen; at the same time he could make his point without question. Unfortunately, each of the reports was consigned to the shelf and allowed to gather dust. The Executive, dust, gave way to corrupt and unscrupulous persons instead of chastising them.

Now during past years due to the spread of education and more active and wary role of the media, people are wide awake to their rights and duties; their unwavering faith in the judiciary, has brought it forward to their grievances through PIL and tried to find solutions to their problems. And the judiciary, too, has never failed them or disappointed them; it has assumed the role of an activist. As a result many tainted sheep have been brought to the dock. To quote Mr.Pathak, "The concept of judicial activism can be seen as the expansion of the rights of judiciary to ensure that the due process of administration is not marred by systematic distortions, including derelection of duty or abuse of power to subvert the system."[1]

Last but not least, at the threshold of independence rather even earlier, the entrance of rampant corruption in politics proved fatal. In 1939 Gandhiji had written in great agony, "I would go to the length of giving the whole Congress organisation a decent burial, rather than put up with the corruption that is rampant."[2] Alas ! none heeded the sagacious warning. Truly speaking when India was in her formative stage, the few guides of the nation adopted self-seeking as a principle and opportunism as a creed. No responsible person could perceive the aftermath of such nasty cases and unscrupulous and unqualified persons began to flourish on the ruins of values in politics, nay, in life. They made no hitch in flouting the laws of the land. They had lost all sense of accountability to the people in the desert of immorality and unscrupulousness. They neglected hopes and aspirations of the people who elected them for a mission — to build up a new nation — prosperous, powerful, self-sufficient, enlightened, free from all evils. The politicians involved themselves in corrupt practices; so their subordinate officials also did not lag behind them. They had a nexus with all sorts of persons who could help them in this foul game-at the nation's cost. Now the wheel of corruption started rolling downwards and the Government employees began to accept

1 An article by B.Pathak; The Hindustan Times; April 28, 1996.

2 Harijan; May 27, 1939.

hush money to get things done. It was very well known to the Government itself but the malady went on without remedy. Dr. Radhakrishnan, the then president, expressed his deep concern over the growing charges of corruption against many high-ups in his message to the nation on Republic Day on 25 January 1967 — "Charges of Corruption are frequently made against people at all levels of Government—Central and state. Immediate disposal of these charges is essential. If these charges are false, their falsehood should be exposed. If there is any basis for them, this should be admitted and rectified."[1] But the Government did not show any enthusiasm for "immediate disposal" of the charges against officials. Therefore, things went on worsening; the responsibility of rectification at any level was not felt. To quote Radhakrishnan again,

"The increase of corruption ..... is due to a considerable extent due to our misplaced kindness and indifference to wrong doing. Maudlin sentimentality is not be confused with generosity or compassion. If we are soft to antisocial wrong doers, we will be doing a great wrong to society."[2] Would the responsible persons heed to the President's warning !

As one wrong begets another, the politicians desired to grab power by hook or by crook. They used both money and muscle to win the election; so they were obliged by businessmen who got undue favour for this kind act.

1 Radhakrishnan's speeches & Writings; Govt. PUblication; p. 86.

2 Ibid; p. 26.

They threw all rules and regulations to the wind to favour their kith and kin. The Apex Court found guilty Ministers of Urban Development Mrs. Sheila Kaul and Mr. P.K. Thungon for alloting houses out-of-turn and Captain Satish Sharma, Petroleum Minister, for distributing petrol pumps from the discretionary quota. While disposing of a public interest petition, ordered to vacate the houses of about 2000 central Government employees and observed, "We hope that the coming years would not see any scam or misuse of power in making allotments of Government quarters. The trust which reposed in this context on high functionaries, would be discharged in accordance with the law."[1] But with the next step the politicians made the court's efforts ineffective and breached the people's trust when 'the Union government issued an ordinance to permit 1,800 out-of-turn allotees to stay. The President Mr. S.D. Sharma who put his signature on the ordinance just one day before the last day given by the supreme court to vacate the houses, and thus endorsed the corrupt practice by high-ups and left 40,000 central Government employees who had been waiting for their turn for a long time to suffer for no fault of theirs. Height of corruption and injustice.

Likewise other politicians, too, misused their power and position to amass wealth indiscriminately; and in this unwarranted act they were assisted by top class officials. Without the least realization all sorts of malpractices — black marketing, hoarding, adulteration, bribery etc. were brought into practice and the defaulters were never dealt with strictly.

1 The Hindustan Times; December 23, 1997.

Dr. Radhakrishnan had lamented the sorry plight of things quite long ago, "A recent report shows that aduteration of food is being practised on a large scale. Of all anti-social practices there is none more heinous than adulteration of food stuff. The practioners of this evil, the hoarders, the profiteers, the marketeers and the speculators are among the worst enemies of our society. They have to be dealt with sternly, however well-placed, important and influential they may be. If we acquiesce in wrong doing, people will lose faith in us."[1] All anti-social evils are not only in practice but also soaring high; the officials are accomplices in this flourishing business and they have the blessings of the political masters. Adulteration of food is in full swing these days. It has claimed the lives of several people. To the horror of people, synthetic milk instead of milk which is a complete diet and necessary for children who are the promise of the future, is available in plenty in the market under the officials' very nose.

As our politicians started getting money from the business-men, they became puppets in their hands and the latter got all that was needed to promote their business. They gained direct or indirect interference in political affairs; and in this foul game, especially the leaders of the ruling party played a vital role and even they staked the security of the country. In one of its judgements the Supreme Court held "we cannot be blind to the fact that even after 50 years of our independence our territorial integrity is not fully secure."[2] True to the core the people of Punjab and Jammu and Kashmir

1 Radhakrishnan's Speeches & Writings; op cit; p. 26.

2 The Times of India; Feb 7, 1997.

have paid heavily due to unsafe boundaries of the country. Today there is hardly any office in the country where corruption does not prevail. Most of the people suffer at the hands of the bureaucrats. They do not get even right things done without paying hush money. This is the worst tragedy in a free country that people have to grease the palms of the public servants to get their rights. Simultaneously, nepotism, favouritism, bribery, negligence of duty, treachery, unemployment, kidnapping, sychophancy and a million of related problems have become a natural phenomenon of the Indian bureaucracy. Common people, unlike in the days of struggle for freedom, have difficult access to the leaders who are the representatives; moreover, there are none to attend to their complaints or to heed their grievances. Of course, they pay lip service to them. Politicians have built up an aura of superiority around them and they break laws as they please for their selfish and petty ends. To quote Mr.Arun Shourie, "The politicians', culture has today begun to infert every institution. It is a misconception that since they are the elected representatives of the people they are superior to everyone else."[1] As a result, briefly speaking, scams and scandals have rocked the nation's progress and the business-politics nexus is flourishing luxuriantly at the cost of the nation.

II. Role of the Judiciary :

Hazy and sleazy atmosphere prevails all over the country. No institution seems to be working smoothly. Every institution

1. The Hindustan Times, Feb 22, 1997; p. 3.

seems to be sick. Both the Executive and Parliament have also failed to discharge "their elementary obligation of ensuring compliance of laws passed by them." "The root is too deep to respond to a surface or isolated treatment. Nor is the malady a localised wound that can be cleaned, disinfected, bandaged and healed by an earnest and eminent surgeon. The cancerous roots, in fact, admit of no such treatment. If removed from one place, they appear at another."[1] The total picture of public life is dismal as well as discouraging. The modus operandi of the public servant cannot be allowed to go on without question. In the words of Mr.J.K. Das, "The unusual speed with which the entire exercise is intended to be hustled through in these days of scams and kickbacks also confirms the worst public fears that all is not well with the Indian polity."[2] People are fed up with this system.

Most of the people are in a dilemma about what to do. They do not know how to break through the net of a corrupt political and bureaucratic system but some daring and optimistic persons knocked at the door of the judiciary to unearth the black deeds of these high-ups and their accomplices. They found a silver lining in the dark clouds when the judiciary responded to their knock. Consequently, many sensational scandals involving both politicians and officials have come to light. To quote a letter published in The Hindustan Times (Dec. 17, 1997) — "There has been so much accumulation of scams and scandals that the moral majority of the country have been placed in a complete morass

1 An article by Mr. Jag Mohan; The Indian Express; Dec. 16, 1996.

2 An article by J.K. Das; Ibid.

of confusion and are gradually becoming unable to distinguish the details of one from those of the other .... the nation is watching with keen interest the ongoing exhibition of scandals and want to see that the guilty are punished according to their deserts ...". Let us have a look at the "exhibition of scandals".

(1) Urea Scam
(2) Hawala Scandal
(3) J.M.M. Pay-off Case
(4) Telecom Scandal
(5) Ayrvedic Scandal
(6) Skipper Case
(7) Madhotal Land Scam
(8) Security Scam
(9) Fodder Scam
(10) Bitumen Scam
(11) Police Uniform
(12) Land Scandal
(13) TV Scam
(14) Gift-Cheque Scam
(15) Alk Tara Scandal (Bihar)
(16) FC I- Wheat Scandal
(17) A.H.D. Appointment Case
(18) H.D.W. Case
(19) Sen Gupta FERA Case
(20) Saint Kitts Forgery Case
(21) Housing Scam
(22) Noida Land Scam
(23) Petrol Pumps Allotment Scam, etc.

The catalogue of corrupt and atrocious deeds defeats its own end. All these scandals involve millions of rupees which have been shared by highly placed persons. There are about 120-125 cases under trial; these cases are such as have drawn people's attention all over the country. Besides, others have not been flashed in headliness of the newspapers while some of them have been disposed of at some level the other or. These scams belong to money matters; there are other corrupt practices such as deprived of their social and economic entitlement or that social legislation enacted for their benefit is not being implemented thus depriving them of the rights and benefits conferred upon them, the court can and must intervene and compel the executive to carry out its constitutional and legal obligations and ensure that the deprived and vulnerable sections of the community are no longer subjected to exploitation or injustice and they are able to realize their social and economic rights."[1]

When the aggrieved party reaches the court, it cannot sit on the fence. Its action never aims at finding fault with the executive or the legislative, but on relieving the people of their suffering. It reminds the executive of its constitutional obligation. It dismisses the mistaken belief of such persons that they are above the law and are accountable to none in the country. "When the Court passes any orders in a public interest litigation, the court does so not with a view to mocking at legislative or executive authority

1 An article by N.H. Hingorani The Statesman; Jan. 1, 1997.

or in a spirit of confrontation but with a view to enforcing the constitution and the law, ..."[1] As a result non-accountability of the representatives; the people who have pinned their faith in them, are robbed of their due share; not to speak of civic amenities which are necessary for a promised better life and a sign of a civilized society. Hon'ble Prime Minister, Shri Rajeev Gandhi, accepting the corruption in public offices, made a profound statement that "only 15 paise of every rupee trickles down to the poor."[2] Referring to Mr. Gandhi's comment on corruption Justice A.M. Ahmadi's remark is worth-quoting, "What a sad commentary on those responsible for eating away the morsel meant for the poor."[3]

The politicians when they raise a hue and cry over the role of the judiciary, are worried about their image, their power and position. The judicial activities assume significance when the misuse of power of the executive is taken into account. To quote Neerja Chowdhury "The politicians today are totally unmindful of norms and the public sentiment about them even with the judiciary breathing down their neck. So hostile is the public climate against them that any judge who gives bail today (to Narasimha Rao or Sukh Ram or those of their biradiri) will be seen to be acting under pressure. Rao today has become a hate symbol because he epitomises the entire political class. The more he is seen as

1 Ibid

2 The Hindustan Times; Feb 14, 1997; p. 24.

3 The Times of India; Feb 18, 1997, p. 13.

trying to get out of the web that is closing in around him, the worse becomes the public perception about him."[1]

It is an instance of the saviour becoming the eater or the hedge eating away its crops. Froideur between the ruler and the ruled. People-deprived, hopeless, affronted, sad, frightened, anxious and confused-took the last resort to the judiciary for the sake of their 'morsel' and honour which is to be expected in a democratic country. No doubt, the judicial edifice gave shelter and discharged well its time honored duty. The politicians attacked the judiciary with hammer and tongs. But the judiciary changed its traditional colour and started working with a broad view and vision. "It is no longer interpreting laws and the constitution. It is now ensuring that the laws of the land are enforced and it is trying to ensure that the executive does not get away with cover-ups."[2]

Justice Ahmadi gives a befitting reply to the angry politicians, "Changing times make it appropriate for laws and courts to adapt themselves to new situations.... courts are not the only guardians of the constitution but are the last resort."[3] The Apex Court within its ambit is trying hard to do 'complete justice' without fear or favour. It has put all matters of exigency on the front burner. It has kept the old adage that justice must be seen to have been done. In fact, judicial activism is a road by which to approach the highways and by-

1. An article by N. Chowdhury, The Stateman; Oct. 7, 1996.
2 Ibid.
3 The Times of India; Feb 18, 1997 p. 13.

laws of justice. The recent judicial activities have created a general awareness among people on the one hand, and it has protected the people's faith in the judiciary from being blown out.

Kudos? to the judiciary that it has risen to the occasion!

CHAPTER SIX

Judicial Activism, Through PIL

In fact, Public Interest Litigation is a "refinement of the legal instruments to ensure speedy dispensation of justice". In today's precarious conditions it has become a powerful means to safeguard the larger good of the public. It is the road to justice-social, political and economic; it is a ray of hope for the deprived, down-trodden and the struggling masses. If the haves have an easy access to the court and the have-nots cannot approach the court, it defies the very spirit of the constitution. Broadening the concept of the PIL Justice Bhagwati has observed, "Where a member of the public acting bonafide moves the Court for enforcement of a fundamental right on behalf of a person or class of persons who on account of poverty or disability or socially or economically disadvantaged position cannot approach the Court for relief, such member of the public may move the Court even by just writing a letter because it would not be right or fair to expect a person acting pro-bono publico to incur expenses out of his own pocket for going to a lawyer and preparing a regular writ petition for being filed in Court for enforcement of the fundamental right of the poor and deprived sections of the community and in such a case, a letter addressed by him can legitimately be regarded as an "apporopriate" proceeding." (Sccp, 187). The concept of the PIL under Art 32 has awakened the people to justice, the rule of law, equality and other ideals which are the backbone of a democratic system. At the abject failure of executive and legislature some public organizations and individuals as well rolled up their sleeves against the onslaught of democratic ideals. To quote Justice Krishna Iyer, "Social justice can never be transformed into a living principle under conditions of penury, disability and primitive privations unless social activists, vigilant expert bodies and crusaders for common causes bring up injustices for judicial redressal. Public Interest Litigation, where the particular party, who moves the court, suffers no personal injury but agitates a grievance common to the community, is a necessary forensic archery in the procedural armoury."[1] PIL is the best and the cheapest means to get justice otherwise it is a mere slogan due to "high cost and complexity of procedure in litigation." It has given an opportunity to the layman to move the court for quick redressal of his grievances. It has indeed, thrown "open the portals of the courts to the common man"; it has shown a silver lining in the dark clouds. If this unfailing weapon of PIL is used with judiciousness and sagacity, it can unlock the doors of justice to the disabled and undermined and can evade the malaise prevailing every where. Justice Bhagwati has observed in no uncertain terms - "Public Interest Litigation is not in the nature of adversary litigation but it is a challenge and an opportunity to the government and its officers to make basic human rights meaningful to the deprived and vulnerable sections of the community and to assure them social and economic justice which is the

1 Iyer Krishnan,, V.R., Social Justice Sunset or Dawn; Eastern Book Company, Lucknow, 1993; p. 151.

signature tune of our constitution. The government and its officers must welcome public interest litigation because it would provide them an occasion to examine whether the poor and the down-trodden are getting their social and economic entitlements or whether they are continuing to remain victims of deception and exploitation at the hands of strong and powerful sections of the community and whether social and economic justice has become a meaningful reality for them or it has remained merely a teasing illusion and a promise of unreality.....". (SCC p. 182).

With the advent and practice of PIL the common man who is condemned to lead a dog's life struggling throughout life in the quest of a dignified place in society, dies like a dog at last and leaves a bitter legacy for his children, feelsat hand the promise of jurisprudence. As a living principle it has emerged with new social rights. It is of paramount importance because it is making law and justice accessible to the millions who are on the verge of losing hope in the system itself. It brings the poor man to the court where he can narrate his woeful tale full of injustice and exploitation. Not only this but PIL is also highly interested in results without losing immeasurable time in marathon arguments making the things more and more complicated. The poor masses have found it suitable to their needs and soothing in their distress. Mr. U.C. Agarwal aptly holds, "since no other credible independent body was available for speedy justice, the Public Interest Litigation (PIL) route was found to be the most convenient way to approach the higher courts."[1]

1. The Hindustan Times, April, 16, 1997.

Again, "In contrast, no forms are prescribed under PIL, no affidavit is required, no fee is involved and there is no fear of punishment if the complaint is not proved. In fact, in important cases of public interest, the burden of investigation is taken over by the courts by utilising the assistance of eminent lawyers as "amicus curiae."[1] These lawyers have surely helped the courts to take up the cases of public interest and hammered at the obstacles in the way to justice when "the courts hauled up senior politicians or government functionaries and even ruled how cases should be investigated and by whom"[2]. By taking up the cases of public interest, the court has kept the lamp of judicial awareness constant and unflickering; and simultaneously it has reasserted that under Act. 21 of the constitution each of the judges is "accountable and answerable to the people for unjustifiable delay in disposing of the cases." The concept of PIL is an humble attempt to defy the old proverb - law governs the poor and the rich govern the law.

Justice Krishna Iyer has dwelt upon the "judicial crusadism" through PIL. He says sagaciously, "Public interest law has many dimensions and limitations and, in its present embryonic state, jurisprudence must take care to formulate sound principles for future development. There is no doubt whatever that tomorrow belongs to public interest law and litigation, but its very importance and critical function call for careful designing and engineering, sketching of limitation and lines of opening. For instance, the massive wrongs and

1. Ibid.

2. Editorial, The Hindustan Times; April, 12, 1997.

injustices of today are a wide range - environmental pollution, ecological crucifixion, social inequities and economic exploitation plus a tremendous variety of crimes - and offer new opportunities for evolution of Indian jurisprudence, processual and substantive."[1]

Public Interest Litigation has invoked the Court in several grey areas. Let us discuss some of them.

1. Expanding Horizons of Locus Standi Rule

In a civilized society "access to justice" is the first and foremost right; the distance between man and justice marks the progress of our culture and civilization as well as the prosperity of our different institutions which aim at making life better. Justice Krishna Iyer has put in candid terms, ".... but when the masses are illiterate, indigent, oppressed and unable to hire counsel or battle against the exotic, expensive legalisties currently besetting the judicial process, traditionally narrow, individualistic rules of locus standi only roadbloc the path to remedial justice."[2] Indeed, law is the measure of civilization. The more we are civilized, the more access freely and fairly we have to justice. The distance between man and justice is abridged and the system is less cumbersome. It helps society move towards the acme of civilization. Realising the gravity of the 'agonising gap between the ideal of equal access and availability of legal justice', the Supreme Court has expanded the horizons of

1 Iyer, Krishna, Social Justice - Sunset or Dawn; Opcit, pp. 153, 154.

2 Ibid.

locus standi rule which is a landmark contribution to India's legal system. It is a revolutionary change which is fairly expected to meet the need of the times. In fact, seeds of its expansion were sown long ago in the year of 1975 in the Dabholkar case but the first courageous step of its 'lucid elaboration' was taken by Justice Krishna Iyer in 1976. In a judgement he observes, "Public interest is promoted by a spacious co3ntruction of Locus standi in our socio-economic circumstances ..... Representative actions, pro bono publico and like ...... are in keeping with the current assent of justice to the common man."[1]

Under thc aegis of Justice P.N. Bhagwati the apex court witnessed the formalisation of the PIL concept and referred to the "Courts of the poor and struggling masses of this country" and opened a new graceful chapter in the legal system in 1982 when he observed, "any member of the public or social action group acting bonafide can invoke the writ jurisdication of the High Courts or the Supreme Court seeking redressal against violation of legal or constitutional rights of persons who owing to social or economic or other disbility cannot approach the court."[2] Indeed, the judgement has gone a long way in making PIL a potent weapon defending against ills in every walk of life. It has prepared a good background for the coming judges to expand locus standi rules to meet new challenges in the years to come. Hence PIL, like a dose of salts.

1. Mumbai Kamgar Sabha V. Abdulbhai, AIR 1976 Sc 1455-1458.
2. S.P. Gupta V Union of India, AIR, 1982 Sc 149 at 188-89 .

2. Evolvement of Epistolary Jurisprudence

It is horrible to think that the poor who are the victims of either the administrative 'heartless insensitivity' or the mafia using them for their own advantage, do not reach the Court by being illiterate, disabled by the complex legal procedure. They have no choice but to live in inhuman conditions which are beyond imagination in civilized society. In order to bridge the gap between man and justice, the Supreme Court has started treating mere letters addressed to it, "as writ petitions in cases involving larger public interest or gross violation of fundamental rights". In the case of Bandhua Mukti Morcha, Justice P.N. Bhagwati has observed -

"Where a member of the public acting bonafide moves the court for enforcement of a fundamental right on behalf of a person or class of persons who on account of poverty or disability .... such member of the public may move the Court even by just writing a letter ...."[1]

Justice A.N. Sen stood by the ruling and observed : "The Supreme court for quite some years now has in many cases proceeded to act on the basis of the letters addressed to it ....." The landmark ruling of the Court has paved the way for the poor, oppressed, illiterate and down-trodden to get justice against any kind of exploitation. Justice Krishna Iyer has hailed the timely step of the Court - "The Supreme Court, realising this social imperative of Third World jurisprudence,

1 See Scc. 189 (1984).

wrought into the system seminal reforms breaking away from hide-bound orthodoxies and precedent - pickled cans of colonial vintage. Thc court under the new radicalism acts on mere letters of litany, ... Epistolary jurisdiction is a judicial innovation responding to the challenges of social justice."[1] Such letters spirited by public interests have relieved bonded labourers, illegal detenus etc. The court has undone many wrongs of violation of human rights. Committed to justice, the Court has come forward to render justice to the common man when it has taken "suomoto cognizance of 'letters to the editor' in newspapers and has granted relief to the aggrieved.

But Justice Krishna Iyer is not satisfied with this expansion. He advises the Court to cover a wide range of things in order to render significant legal service to the people. He avers in clear-cut terms, "The jurisdictional expansion imparted by this dynamic jurisprudence cannot be of much avail to the humbler brackets of the community unless the highest court is ready to adopt new canons of interpretation which will vitalise the words of the Constitution and the laws and rescue those who are suppressed and oppressed by anti-social forces."[2]

We fondly hope the court should heed these words above!

1 Iyer, Krishna; Social Justice-Sunset or Dawn - Opcit, pp 149-150.

2 Ibid, p. 153.

3. Appointment of Socio-legal Commissions

Casual justice is no justice at all. For complete realisation of justice the Supreme Court has made no hitch in departing from "its adversarial method prevailing hitherto" and "resorted to inquisitional method in PIL matters." Therefore, it has gone to the length of appointing commissions from among eminent as well as enlightened advocates, professors, magistrates, journalists or other sensitive persons for collecting facts and figures in PIL cases. These commissions have helped the court to a great extent to arrive at a logical conclusion in order to grant relief to the oppressed. To quote Justice Krishna Iyer, "Indeed, prison justice, liberation of bonded labour, punitive action against blindings of prisoners and excessive detention by State agencies securing the rights of workers when welfare laws are violated, ... these and other unconventional yet critical, reliefs have been rendered by the Indian courts."[1] In the case of the Bhagalpur prisoners[2] who were blinded, the court appointed eye - specialists to 'ascertain the nature of harm' done to them. Similarly to know exactly the working conditions in stone - quarries of Faridabad a sociologist was sent there as commissioner.

Thus, the common man and the court have come close and public interests are predominant. The commissions appointed by the Court, have made the things which were convoluted, crystal clear. The court has treated these cases

1 Ibid, p. 13.

2 Khatri V State of Bihar, AIR 1981 Sc 928.

in exigency so that the underprivileged may not suffer any longer. The timely step of the court has saved the lives of millions from becoming hellish.

4. Monitoring Laws and Judicial orders

In many cases the court has found bureaucratic lethargy and laxity as a great hurdle in the way to justice. Either the investigating agencies have not done their home work well, conscientionsly or delayed under one pretext or the other. Consequently, the culprits have fair chances to go scot free. Justice J.S. Verma observed in the Hawala case that "investigating agencies had not done a satisfactory job in probing the case, otherwise it would not have been possible for all the chargesheets to end up in a fiasco."[1] Again, "It appears clear now that they only put up an excuse of filing a chargesheet because if the discharge of the accused is justified then apparently there was no prima facie case put up along with the chargesheet for the trial to commence."[2] The courts have hauled up the investigating agencies many times for tardy investigation. It seems that these inquiring agencies either work under pressures of big bosses or connive with the accused. They file chargesheets without proper investigation or the investigation is improper. The court is helpless to bring the accused to book. It is necessary for the courts to vilify these agencies so they "have themselves monitored CBI investigations, their own orders/directions and have been monitoring anti-pollution laws etc."[3]

1 The Hindustan Times, Aug. 29, 1998.

2 Ibid.

3 Indian Council for Enviro-Legal Action V Union of India (1996), 55 CC 281.

Here the courts, besides interpreting laws and the constitution, have to ensure that the laws of the land are enforced. The Patna High Court has pulled up the CBI joint Director Biswas for sending his report to Delhi. "It was the court which had ordered that Biswas continue with the case, as observes Neerja Chowdhury. "It was the court - and not the State government - which had ordered the inquiry to be conducted by the CBI and they did not even route the request through the State Government."[1] The Apex Court had to order the CBI to report to the Court itself in many cases. For this action the court has been severely criticised in many quarters of intellectuals but it has been widely acclaimed by the public. But, it gave a wide spectrum to judicial activities.

5. Enforcing Public Duties

It is a profound rather than the prominent duty of the Courts to keep the other organs of the Government. active and within constitutional bounds and "to perform their affirmative constitutional / statutory obligations". Justice Krishna Iyer opines "What is most important is that justice to the people is not a matter solely for courts and judges or for lawyers and litigants; it is deeper and more pervasive and its instrumentalities include law-making professionals, paralegislative operators, enforcement agencies and the central actors, viz, legislative, judicative and executive institutions and their personnel."[2] No apex court works in an ivory tower; but it has to see if the other wings of the

1 The Indian Express. Oct. 7, 1996.

2 Iyer, Krishna, Social Justice - Sunset or Dawn; Op cit, p. 37.

Government discharge their duties in consonance with the constitution for complete justice. Fiasco on the part of the executive in response to people's grievances, the courts have to direct the other organ as the final authority. "If the judiciary has been more involved in public interest litigation than before, it is because the executive's actions have not always been seen to be above board."[1]

The Court does not intend to find fault with the legislative or the executive, but when public interest or justice is jeopardized, it has to step in. In a case relating to bonded labour, which is prohibited by the constitution, the Apex court reiterated that "if the executive is not carrying out any duty laid upon it by the constitution or the law, the court can certainly require the executive to carry out such duty."[2] And this is exactly what the courts do when they entertain public interest litigation. Again - "When the Court passes any orders in a public interest litigation the Court does so not with a view to mocking at legislative or executive authority or in a spirit of confrontation but with a view to enforcing the constitution and the law, because it is vital for the maintenance of the rule of law that the obligations which are laid upon the executive by the constitution and the law should be carried out faithfully and no one should go away with a feeling that the constitution and the law are meant only for the benefit of a fortunate few and have no meaning for the large numbers of half-clad, half hungry people of the country."[3]

1 Editorial, The Hindustan Times; Aug. 21, 1998.

2 The Statesman (Jan. 9, 1997) Judicial Activism I by N.H. Hingorani.

3 Ibid.

Thus, in many PIL cases the courts have issued orders and directions to enforce duties; eg. on sanitation[1] environmental protection[2], labour welfare[3], investigation by police or CBI[4] and human rights[5].

Besides, entertaining a PIL division bench of the Apex court, Justice A.S. Anand and Justice V.N. Khare while adjourning hearing on three public interest petitions challenging construction on safety grounds, granted three month's time to the central and Uttar Pradesh Government to finalise follow up action (H.T. July 23, 1998); other two petitions include Almatic dam and the Kaveri dispute.

Acting on a writ petition regarding lawlessness prevailing in Delhi, a division bench (Delhi High Court) comprising acting Chief Justice Mahinder Narain and Justice S.K. Mahajan in its order said, "We would like to know from the respondents (Centre, Delhi Government and Police Commissioner) what action is being taken in view of the state of lawlessness which seems to have affected the national capital territory (H.T. July 24, 1998).

1 Dr. B.L. Wadhera V Union of INdia, AIR, 1996, Sc 2969.

2 M.C. Mehta V Union of India (1996) 4 SEc 750.

3 Supra n 3 and n 9.

4 Vineet Narayan V Union of India AIR 1996 Sc 3386.

5 Supra n 14 and 11

In a significant order, the Indore Bench of the Madhya Pradesh High Court has directed the State Government to take decision within a month on the Keer Committee recommendations for providing relief to the families of those killed in the 1984 anti Sikh-riots. The bench gave the direction on a public interest litigation. The court said that if the State Government failed to take a decision, it would have to pay an additional amount of Rs.50,000 and provide Rs.100,000 each to the families of those killed in the riots (The Indian Express, Sept. 3, 1998).

6. Area of PIL

In fact, it is widely realised that certain inherent problems, indiscipline and interference of higher ups and politicians have made the present system ineffective. People have lost faith in it and are constrained to approach the court which entertains a PIL as writ jurisdiction conferred by Articles 32 and 226 respectively of the constitution and "these articles impose a positive constitutional obligation on the Court to enforce fundamental rights of citizens." At the same time people have begun to realise that PIL is not a panacea. As Justice Verma opines the role of courts while dealing with PIL is to ensure that the authorities perform their statutory function and not to restrain them from performing their jobs. It is true that "the courts, needless to say, should not be taken as a final solution. They act only as catalyst and draw attention to the problem."[1]

1 The Times of India (Aug. 12, 1997) PIL : The Flipside- by Rakesh Bhatnagar.

Nevertheless, a benign contribution of the courts in many grey areas which have been brought within the bosom of judiciary, cannot be gainsaid. It has helped evolve jurisprudence to relieve the oppressed as well as to bring the layman near the justice which was a distant dream for them due to heavy expenses and legal complications. The critics of "judicial activism" who hold that the judges "have lately shown a disturbing tendency to encroach on the executive domain", denounce PIL as a menace while others are of the opinion that the court has enlarged the scope of Article 32. In recent years the courts have passed many directives of vital importance on a variety of issues. Let us discuss those grey areas which were thought to be alien earlier to the judiciary.

Prisoner's Rights and Prison administration

The Apex Court has upheld prisoners and detenus' rights to speedy trial[1], free legal aid, dignified treatment[2] and rights against illegal detention[3], custodial death and torture[4] etc. In 1979, a Supreme Court lawyer came upon an article published in the Indian Express by K.F. Rustamji, a member of the Police Commission who gave a lurid account of the undertrial prisoners in the jails of Bihar. There were a large number of men, women and children for minor offences in the different prisons for as many as 20 years without their

1 Hussainara Khatoon V. State of Bihar, AIR 1979 Sc 1369.

2 Rama Murthy V State of Karnataka, AIR 1997 Sc 1997, 1739.

3 Ms. Veena Sethi V State of Bihar, AIR 1983 Sc 339.

4 D.K. Basu V. State of West Bengal, AIR 1997 Sc 610.

trials having even started. Most of these prisoners were too poor to afford their bail and the courts were overloaded due to being understaffed. This socially spirited lawyer filed the first ever public interest litigation in the Supreme Court, "Without any power of attorney but on the basis of the published article, on behalf of some of the undertrials, Hussainara Khatoon and 12 others, bringing to the notice of the Supreme Court their continued detention in violation of their fundamental right under Article 21 of the constitution in view of the section 428 of the code of Criminal Procedure — for, even if the said prisoners had been tried and convicted of the offences charged, they would have been released years ago after serving their sentences."[1]

The court entertained the PIL and passed the order for immediate release of these prisoners. As a result about 40,000 prisoners were released in Bihar on personal or no bond. It was a different PIL from the traditional ones. The concept of a PIL has been well set up by the subsequent matters entertained by the Apex Court in the case of the Bhagalpur blindings and the Rudul Sah's case. The nature, scope and limitation of a PIL is clearly expressed by the Apex Court in a case relating to employment of children in hazardous industries in spite of the constitutional prohibition.

The Court categorically held invalid and unconstitutional the incarceration of "children in jails instead

1 The Statesman - Judicial Activism - I by N.H. Hingorani, Jan. 1, 1997.

of remand homes,[1] and imprisoning of non-criminal insane persons."[2] The Supreme Court has recently laid down detailed guidelines-cum requirements for arrest and detention of persons.[3]

Protection of bonded, Contract and child labour

To begin with Justice Krishna Iyer remarks, "The tribals, for instance, have been cheated and schemes for their benefit are avid opportunities for corruption with the voiceless being still exploited so also the Harijans. Bonded labour is abolished by law but abounds in fact. .... The children of Sivakasi are exploited from dawn to dusk with no right to sing or play or read and write, save to starve in a deadly industry heedless of the laws and the constitution."[4] In such shameful cases when the moral fibre of the tycoons is dead due to greed and callousness, the court's conscience is pricked and it stands by these hapless, illiterate and suppressed persons. The court entertained fervently PIL cases addressing the plight of the labour class and granted relief[5] and ensured better enforcement of various labour laws. In PIL cases the court is led to believe that the larger public interest must outweigh an individual's personal interest; it promotes probity in public life. To the weak and vulnerable sections of our society the Supreme Court stands like a tower of strength in times of

1 Sheela Barse V Union of India, AIR 1986 Sc 1973.

2 Sheela Barse V Union of India 1993 AIR Sc W 2908.

3 D.K. Basu V State of West Bengal, AIR 1997, Sc 610.

4 Iyer Krishna, Social Justice - Sunset or Dawn; op cit, p. 146-47.

5 Neeraja Chaudhary V State of M.P. AIR 1984 Sc 1099.

crisis and paves the way when nothing is seen in the darkness of corruption, cruelities callousness and cantrip. The court has come to their rescue, when heaps of legislation have failed to relieve them of inhuman conditions in which they are forced to earn their livelihood. The interpretation made by the court is to meet the new challenges of the time; and, of course, it has done a laudable job by abolishing child labour which is a slur on the fair face of our civilized society.

Expansion of Right to Life

While interpreting Article 21 which gives all citizens the right to life, the Supreme Court has said : "We think that the right to life includes the right to live with basic human dignity and all that goes along with it, namely the bare necessities of life such as adequate nutrition, clothing and shelter over the head and facilities for reading, writing and expressing oneself in diverse forms."[1] Indeed the right to life is the most comprehensive human right in a free and civilized society. It promises the all round development of man. It lends beauty, dignity and grace to life. It aims at both mental and physical development. All conditions which help man grow luxuriantly must be fulfilled in society if it is to be a civilized and cultured one.

Emphasising the right to life Justice Krishna Iyer opines "I would prefer the expression "right to live". I do

1 Mainstream, Vol. XXIV No. 28 - March 15, 1986, p. 12.

not want any people just to survive. I want them to live a life of human dignity and, for that, they must have the basic necessities of life including food and health. The right to life in my opinion includes right to basic necessities of life. One of the major events in the judicial history of India has been the fuller exploration of the right to life guaranteed under. 21 of the constitution. This right is not merely lexical and legal, but expands as we conceptualise the dignity and divinity of the human personality."[1]

With the full conceptualisation of the human personality the Supreme Court has included 'finer graces of human civilization[2] to the right to life. Thus, it includes right to live with human dignity,[3] right to healthy environment,[4] free education upto 14 years of age[5], emergency medical aid[6], privacy[7] et all. If there is a violation of any such right, the responsible person is liable to compensation or exemplary penalty. Thus, the court has made efforts to provide an ethical atmosphere for the citizens of India.

1 Iyer, Krishna, Social Justice - Sunset or Dawn; Op cit, pp. 15-16.

2 P. Nalla Chandhari V. Union of INdia, AIR 1986, Sc 1133.

3 Francis Coralic v. Administrator, Union Territory of Delhi AIR 1981 Sc 746.

4 M.C. Mehtare V. Union of India AIR 1987 Sc 1086 at P. 1090.

5 J.P. Unnikrishnan V. State of Andhra Pradesh, AIR 1993 Sc 2178.

6 Pramanand Kataria V. Union of India, AIR 1989 Sc 2039.

7 Peoples' Union of Civil Liberties V. Union of India, AIR 1997 Sc 568.

Protection of Environment

The Supreme court in M.C. Mehta V. Union of India[1] has observed "There is also one other matter to which we should like to draw the attention of the Government of India. We have noticed that in the past few years there is an increasing trend in the number of cases based on environmental pollution and ecological destruction coming up before the courts. Many such cases concerning the material basis of livelihood of millions of poor people are reaching this court by way of public interest litigation."

Of course, a healthy environment is indispensable for a better life. Hence, to protect environment and public health is a constitutional obligation of the state[2]. It is a sad commentary on the part of the Government that a number of anti-pollution laws have proved ineffective and environmental pollution still persists in menacing public health alarmingly. The Apex Court as guardian of citizens fundamental rights has stepped in through PIL to ensure vigorous enforcement of these laws. Consequently, many industries polluting environment and endangering public health were ordered to be shifted. The court banned felling of trees in forests. It also put a curb on the running of saw mills and mining in forest areas. The State was declared bound to protect all natural

1 1986 2 Sec 176. 201-02.

2 Vineet Naryan V Union of India, AIR 1996 Sc 3386

resources of public use, as their trustee. 'Accepting sustainable development' as part of customary international law, the court declared 'polluter pays' principle as a part of Indian environmental law and imposed damages on polluting industries.[1]

Political Corruption and Crime

Many PIL cases have unearthed corrupt and criminal activities of the politicians who betrayed the millions of people of this country who pinned their innocent faith in their leadership hoping that they would give them a better life. The holistic truth of 'tryst with destiny' has proved a cry in the wilderness, and the odyssey for a better life has turned out to be a nightmare. We are deprived of 'finer graces' of civilization by our own people whom we think of as saviours, law-makers. Let us see what Neerja Chowdhury thinks about today's politicians - "The politicians today are being unmindful of norms and the public sentiment about them even with the judiciary breathing down their neck. So hostile is the public climate against them that any judge who gives bail today (to Narsimha Rao or Sukhram or those of their 'biradiri) will be seen to be acting under pressure."[2] The situation is degenerating day by day; now the rhetorical words of these politicians seem to be irksome. The assessment about the present scenario made by Bindeswar

1 Indian Council for Enviro-Legal Action V. Union of India, (1996) 5 Sec. 281.

2 The Indian Express (Oct. 7, 1996) Long arm of the law ill finally take its course.

Pathak in his article is true to the core - "The weakening of administration following loss of surrender of constitutional responsibility by bureaucrats has resulted in an unholy alliance between the criminals and politicians, the result of which is there for all to see. What we see by way of a series of scams, are only the tips of the iceberg; the pervasive corruption, breakdown of law and order...."[1]

To put a restraint on the abuse of public power the court has discharged its duty sincerely and invalidated misuse of discretionary power "with imposing of exemplary damages in 'Housing scam'[2] and 'Petrol Pump Scam' case[3]" The Court itself monitored CBI investigations as they were not being carried fearlessly, in the Fodder scam case, where prosecution proceedings on a former CM were unreasonably withdrawn or where a State Government indulged routinely in repromulgation of ordinances thereby usurping legislative function[4], the Court struck down such acts as illegal or unconstitutional. The Court laid down directions that in such cases 'every citizen'[5] has locus standi to move the higher courts to indicate public interest.

Whenever, the courts pronounced judgement in political matters, the lobby of politicians and bureaucrats

1 The Hindustan Times (April 28, 1996) It's right, My Lord by B. Pathak.

2 Shiv Sagar Tewari V Union of India AIR 1997 Sc 2725.

3 Common cause V Union of India AIR 1997 Sc 1886.

4 Sheonandan Paswan V State of Bihar, AIR 1987 Sc 877.

5 Ibid.

raised their eye brows - "unfortunately this has become something of a grey area ever since an activist judiciary, responding to various public interest petitions, has been encroaching into administrative and other fields which have always been the sole responsibility of the government."[1]

Miscellaneous cases

It is true that the court does not rule over the country but its hawk-eyed observation can see the governance of the country. Being committed to the rule of law, it steps in to set things right in case the rule of law is threatened. When the U.P. governor dismissed the Kalyan Singh government and appointed Mr. Jagdambika Pal the Chief Minister over night, the Allahabad High Court gave an interim order which "expressed the view that the question of confidence should have been tested on the floor of the House. Further, by restoring the status quo ante pending the final disposal of the writ petition, the high court virtually nullified the Governor's action."[2] Mr. Jagdambika Pal moved the Supreme Court which "declined to stay the high court's order but then proceeded to modify it significantly by bracketing both Mr. Kalyan Singh and Mr. Jagdambika Pal as contenders for the confidence of the House."[3] It prescribed a composite floor test to avoid

1 The Hindustan Times - editorial; Aug. 21, 1998.

2 The Times of India (March 18, 1998) Courting Confusion by Ramaswamy R Iyer.

3 Ibid.

any confrontation between the two chief Ministers. The court also warned that serious consequences would follow in the event of breach of peace or disturbance during the session. Of course, it was a bizarre problem but the court resolved it and put democracy back on its rails.

"The Cavery water dispute", as the Hindustan Times observes, "has been meandering on for so long that it has come to be recognised as a festering sore in our federal polity."[1] The dispute has actually been politicised and the leaders have not risen above petty political selfish ends to come to terms. "It is this pandering to parochial elements and the politics of pressure tactics in both Tamil Nadu and Karnataka that have frustrated all efforts to find an amicable solution."[2] The matter was brought before the Supreme Court; the concerned parties have sought as many as nine adjournments hoping that they will arrive at a mutual solution but every time vested interests outweighed the national and no breakthrough was made. The Court realised the flashpoint of the dispute and gave three week's time to the Vajpayee Government to solve the long standing dispute. At the direction of the court the Central Government had brainstomring meetings with the two States and reached the amicable solution which was submitted to the court which approved, thinking it beneficial in the interest of the two states. The court's intervention resolved the dispute once and for all.

1. The Hindustan times - July 23, 1998.

2. Ibid.

Probability of PIL's Abuse

On Aug. 8, 1997 while inaugurating the All India Lawyers Convention in Delhi Mr. I. K. Gujral expressed the possibility of the "misuse" of Public Interest Litigation. The posssibility expressed by the then Prime Minister may be due to the "recent instances where the courts had hauled senior politicians or government functionaries and even ruled how cases should be investigated and by whom,"[1] but his doubt is not wholly baseless. In fact, PIL has liberalised locus standi rule and evolved epistolary jurisprudence. And herein lies "dangers of abuse of PIL by vested insterests impelled by personal vendetta, media-craze or other dubious motives."[2] It has become a matter of being extra-careful and meticulous to scrutinze bonafides of the petitioners who should not be allowed to delve into areas where they ought not to tread. In such messy situations the courts have to winnow genuine and real from frivolous and fake petitions. Surely, such abuse not only 'criminally wastes the valuable time of the court'[3] but also creates a 'bottleneck in the superior court[4], preventing other genuine cases from being entertained.

In fact, the Apex court itself, while enlarging the scope of Article 32 which entitles a citizen to seek its

1 Ibid Aug. 12, 1998.

2 AIR 1998, p. 122.

3 Janta Dal V H.S. Chaudhary, AIR 1993 Sc 892.

4 Chhetriya Pradushan Mukti Sangharsh Samiti V State of U.P. AIR 1990 Sc 2060.

intervention, had warned clearly against abuse of PIL. To save valuable time of the courts, self-restraint is suggested in both entertaining and deciding PIL cases. Truly PIL is not the nest for all the bees in the bonnets of public spirited persons.[1] That's why, in certain cases filed in the "public interest" the litigants have failed in evoking positive response as their intention was to settle personal scores. Thus, petition seeking preservation of disputed shrines of Mathura and Kashi was summarily rejected[2], as was the one seeking creation of a new state of 'Telengana' out of Andhra Pradesh[3], and another seeking prohibition on power-cuts depriving cricket fans from watching world-cup tournaments' telecast[4] et al.

To quote the Hindustan Times, "certainly, the finer points of justice and the larger good inherent in PIL would be ill at ease with a situation where the arrears of cases had piled up to cover three crores. The legal process has become excruciatingly time consuming and dilatory and free legal aid to the poor is almost non-existent. While PIL invariably managed to receive prompt attention from the courts and the media, the poor and indigent people locked in litigation continue to suffer in silence."[5] True there is a flip side. The PIL cases have created the problem of huge pendency in the

1 R.S. Sodhi V. State of U.P. 1994 Supp (1) Sec 142.

2 Mohd. Aslam V. Union of India, (1994) 2 Sec 48.

3 Mechineni Krishan Rao V. Union of India AIR 1997 Andh. Pra. 275.

4 K.M. Natraj V State of Karnatak, AIR 1997 Kant-36.

5 The Hindustan Times - Aug. 12, 1997.

courts. If not today, tomorrow people will raise their voices "to end the malaise of continued adjournments of cases which have contributed in large measure to the vast accumulation of backlog of about two crore civil cases and one lakh criminal cases in the courts of India."[1] Such frivolous situations mar the image of the judiciary of providing justice to the people and discharging its responsibilities. In fact, what is the desideratum today in the judiciary is versatile mechanism.

Under constitutional obligation the court has a sacred duty to strike down anc arbitrary or unconstitutional act of other institutions in order to provide relief to the aggrieved party. Even the court can go to the length of evolving new principles for the larger interest or good; and this should not be a matter of objection. The courts have dealt sternly with the matters of corruption and other offences even against MPs, MLAs, Ministers and Governors. It has upset the high-ups. Political resentment is at work against PIL when a Bill to bridle the judiciary has been brought in the 11th Lok Sabha embodying a provision for a forfeitable security of Rs. one lakh with every PIL petition except those by persons below poverty line."[2] Such an act if successful retards the assertion of vindication of citizens' fundamental rights under Arts 32 and 226 of the constitution.

1 The Times of India (Aug. 12, 1998) Clogged Courts : Cases backlog can be cleared - by H.D. Shourie.

2. AIR 1998; p. 172.

The law makers must be wise enough to give up such confrontationist attitude and must join PIL as a participatory venture with the Courts. Hence, no vandalism would be necessary.

CHAPTER SEVEN

Grey Areas of Judicial Activism

What Justice Holmes said, "The prophecy of what the courts will do in fact, and nothing more pretentious is what I mean by the law," is applicable to the Indian Judiciary in the present precarious circumstances. Today it is the most dynamic organ of the Government when other organs — the legislature and the executive, wheel and deal while walking away from the people's primary interests It has wangled itself a favour of the millions of down-trodden and underprivileged people, by keeping the wheel of justice rolling. To quote Justice H.R. Khanna "A judicial system normally represents the transformation of the ideal of rule of law and the yearning for justice into concrete shape. The destiny of each of us in the world of law, of the practising lawyers and of those on the Bench, is linked with our judicial system."[1] It goes without saying that the judiciary has taken a giant leap in the judicial quest for a more humane rule. It has handled the cases sagaciously with courage and confidence. It has pronounced judgements without fear or favour in the fields which were thought to be alien to the judiciary; and the judgements have gone a long way to ensure the rule of law. Again Justice Khanna comments, "The image of the courts in the ultimate analysis depends not upon the architectural beauty and spaciousness of the court buildings. It also does not depend

1 AIR Dec. 1998, p. 195.

upon the long arguments, the number of authorities cited and the erudition displayed in judgements, important though they are. It depends essentially upon the way the cases are handled, upon the extent of the confidence that the courts inspire in the parties that bring cases before them, upon the promptness or absence of delay in the disposal of cases, upon the approximation of the judicial finding of fact with the realities of the matter, we must remember that in the final analysis, the people are the judge of judges and every trial is a trial of our judicial system."[1] Of course, here lies the image and success of our judicial system.

Judicial dynamism lies not so much in what the court says but in what it does with a view "to enhance the utility of that legislation for social betterment." Justice Khanna opines, "Its strength and weakness, its success and failure, its utility and credibility as a necessary organ of the state in a civilized society, the respect it would evoke and the confidence it would inspire would depend ultimately upon the way it satisfies the hopes and aspiration of the people, of the common man in the quest for justice, in keeping the scales even in any legal combat between the rich and the poor, between the mighty and the weak, between the State and the citizen, without fear or favour."[2] Hon'ble Justice is absolutely correct in his assessment. Undoubtedly the Indian Court has enriched the judicial lexicon which will be helpful for the courts in facing new challenges in the years to come but still it has miles to

1 Ibid pp. 195-96.

2 Ibid p. 196.

go to 'do complete justice.' It should not let the grass grow under its feet when it finds injustice in any vulnerable section of society.

Judicial Reforms

Of course, 'petty done, undone vast' must be our watchword. There are many grey areas to unearth where the judiciary has to step in not 'for running its show' or encroaching upon other organs of the Government but because it is the demand of the time. To quote Justice H.R. Khanna, "There is astir today a spirit of scepticism and to some extent iconoclasm. There is much greater awareness of rights and people are acquiring a new consciousness of the strong points and shortcomings of the different human institutions. Many of us in the world of law have so far been unduly allergic to criticism."[1] No one should be allowed to fetter the rights of the underprivileged; they should be given all that they need for a better and peaceful life in a civilized society. For this purpose the judicial system itself needs reforms which will enable our legal system to work more effectively. People who are unaware of the intricacies and perplexities of legal procedures, are far away from justice; if they get it, it is too late for any use. Sometimes in this constant tiresome battle in the Court they get frustrated and lose it like other fields of life. President K.R. Narayanan, inaugurating an all India Seminar on "Judicial Reforms" called for simplifying legal procedures "as part of judicial reforms to ensure speedy

1 Ibid, p. 196.

disposal of cases and reduce mounting litigation costs so that justice is not denied to the people."

Indeed, the judiciary which is the most important pillar in a democratic set-up, needs reforms-radical reforms to meet people's aspirations in the present time of psychological inventions and scientific discoveries which aim at new horizons in every walk of life. Today's man is more aware and enlightened than ever before; so the judiciary is the right place where his feelings can be understood in a better way. If people, in a society like ours where many things are taking shape, are more aware than ever of their rights and duties, living conditions and worried about their future, it is a healthy sign. A new era is assured but if at the dawn of their awakening they are not encouraged to pull together, they are not guided carefully, the new civilized society will be born crippled. Hence, pull all the stops out. At this critical point when other institutions are playing fast and loose, only the judiciary can do a commendable job by dispensing justice to all. Justice H.R. Khanna has come out with a sagacious suggestion. - "The trouble arises when one wing of the state tries to encroach upon the field of the other. It is in the above context that special responsibility develops upon the Judges to avoid the over-activist role and to ensure that they do not overstep or trespass upon the sphere earmarked for the other wings of the State. In certain situations the appeal has to be to the legislature or the executive and the Judges ought not to be reduced by quixotic temptations to encroach upon other fields to set right every fancied wrong paraded before them."[1]

1 Ibid p. 200.

President K.R. Narayanan has aptly observed, "the intricacies of procedures, the ingenuity of lawyers in prolonging cases, even the indifferences of judges and the unending process of appeal that was available had made law a time consuming process."[1] Of course, the President has noted the grievances of the common man who knocks at the door of the court hoping to get justice but it becomes a never-ending game of hide and seek. "The ingenuity of lawyers" is one of the major factors that deludes the common man. The lawyers exercise their influence in the courts and prolong the case if they find that they are going to lose it. They are unaware of the problems of their clients; they go on to continue the battle and keep the client under delusion. Some lawyers have an aura around them of their influence that in most of the subordinate courts "the judges are most reluctant to offend the more successful advocates practising before them. I have known many cases where judges have waited in their chamber for the senior advocate to turn up. Though, in 1966, the Civil Procedure code was amended to provide that adjournments should not be granted to accommodate advocates, the provision has remained a dead letter."[2]

Again, "Advocates blithely ask for adjournments to suit their convenience; the opposing advocate does not object as he knows that there will be a time when he wants an adjournment. Thus, matters get adjourned repeatedly so that advocates can

1 The Hindustan Times; Dec. 6, 1998

2 An article "System that denies justice" by Atul M. Setalvad, The Hindustan Times; Dec. 7, 1998.

move from court to court making the maximum amount of money and the only sufferers are the clients."[1] They hold faithfully 'scratch my back and I will scratch yours.'

Second, "the indifference of judges", the unbelievable but bitter truth of the courts, is a significant point. The President has voiced the needs of the vulnerable millions of India by raising the point. People who turn up for justice with unflagging faith in the system, are betrayed. Justice A.S. Anand has admitted the very fact, "failure of judiciary to deliver justice within a time frame had brought about a sense of frustration among litigants."[2] He has further maintained that the administrative institutions have failed to monitor the status, substance and pace of litigation in courts. It is often observed with wonder and shock that in some cases judgesscarcely bother to know the truth by going into details of a case and they pass judgement quite unmindful of judicial rules which does not appear a judicious judgement but the sweeping comment of a layman. President Narayanan has referred to a case of a five-year-old girl child who had been sexually assaulted by her mother's boy friend, in which, as it was reported, the judge observed that "the child was an unusually promiscuous young lady." Similarly, in the case of Mr. Kalpnath Rai the Apex Court reprimanded the TADA Court Judge Mr.S.N. Dhingra by observing that "Mr. Dhingra had not taken into account certain basic principles of criminal jurisprudence in arriving at conclusions about a dismissed

1 Ibid.

2 The Hindustan Times, Dec. 6, 1998.

officer of the Indian Police Service and about the role of the former Minister in harbouring terrorists."[1] The apex court found the evidence on record on both these points wanting in substance. Of course, judges must decide cases on actual evidence and points of law rather than on perceptions of guilt of the person in public life.' What nearly 400 years ago Francis Bacon, judge and essayist said, must be kept carefully in mind, "if we do not maintain justice, then justice will not maintain us."

The Judiciary must, as the French thinker, Michael Foucault once said, "always question itself."

Moreover, the archaic laws do not serve the purpose in today's changing circumstances. They have failed to a great extent to provide succour to hapless persons. Today people face problems quite different from that of decades ago. Hence, to meet new challenges hurled by new emerging complicated conditions, old laws must be replaced by new dynamic ones. Laws and institutions constantly tend to vegetate, said the U.S. Lawyer, Henry W. Bitchier, "and like clocks, they must be occasionally cleansed, wound up and set to true time." Such evolution of the law will certainly be helpful in non-traditional areas which earlier were considered beyond judicial purview. Justice A. S. Anand favours such evolution and has observed, "what might appear to be non-traditional at the time of the performance of such a task by the judiciary, when considered in proper perspective might

1. Ibid; April 12, 1997.

turn out to be really the process of development of law to respond to the need of the society."[1]

Commenting about our archaic laws Mr. Ravindra Mohan Bagai, a prominent lawyer, says, "Most of our laws are more than a century old and have been copied from the British laws. To meet the present requirements and socio-economic changes a radical revaluation of the old laws is required."[2] Such old mouldy and obsolete laws proved insufficient to lend dignity and grace to human life. Keeping social, economic and political context in mind these laws should be replaced. Without new comprehensive provisions in today's society the quest for justice will be a wild goose chase.*

* "Archaic legal provisions dealing with interim maintenance for separated wives, children and parents are acting as a barrier in providing succour to a hapless woman and her two minor children, Take the case of Manju, her saga began one-one a-half years ago when she had to leave her husband's house following abuse and humiliation. She came back to her widowed mother carrying two minor daughters with her. Soon her husband filed a divorce suit against her stating various grounds including irreconcilable differences. In order to maintain a living, Manju filed a suit seeking interim maintenance of Rs.500/- each per month for herself and her daughters.

According to section 125 of the Code of Criminal Procedure, 1973 which deals with order for maintenance of wives, children and parents, the interim maintenance cannot exceed more than Rs.500/- per month per person.

1. The Hindustan Times, Oct. 30, 1998.
2. Ibid; Dec 14,1998

After deliyberating on the issue for more than a year, the court directed Manju's husband to pay Rs.400/- each as interim relief to her and her daughters till the divorce proceedings were over. Her husband went to a superior court against the order stating that the court had overlooked certain factors like his accident and his family's total income.

The case of Manju ***(see foot note)*** has illustrated the uselessness of old laws "meant to protect and provide succour to the people". It is not an isolated case where old and antiquated laws have failed to bring hope to people's lives. Recently, both the President and the Chief Justice of India Dr.A.S. Anand, in a seminar on 'Judicial Reforms' have laid stress on the immediate need to overhaul old and obsolete laws and legal provisions that have lost their lustre. Besides, many legal experts as well as the Union Law Minister, M. Thambidurai, have realised an imperative need of "scrapping old laws or bringing radical reforms."

In fact, comprehensive steps are necessary for quick justice in the wake of mounting pressure on the institutions of justice. Justice A.S. Anand has rightly put it, "We have not so far succeeded in developing any effective mechanism for the pre-trial settlement of legal dispute, with the result that there is a heavy inflow of all sorts civil, commercial and criminal matters into courts."[1]

The superior court in its order directed that the maintenance allowance should be kept at a total of Rs.700/- (Rs.400/- for Manju and Rs.150/- each for her daughter) reducing it from the earlier total Rs.1200/-. The court also noted that the sum was not enough to meet Manju and her daughters bare needs, but it expressed its inability to do anything....." - A Report by Utpal Paraskar; The Hindustan Times; Dec. 14, 1998.

1 The Hindustan Times, Dec. 13, 1998.

It is a good sign that the judiciary itself is fully aware of the shortcomings of our legal system. Circumstances are well judged and the initiative if taken in time is well worth it.

Delay and Denial of Justice

To begin with the observation of the Times of India (Dec. 15, 1998) "The ringing truth, therefore, is that time is of the essence in delivering justice in any democratic society. Wages say that periodic 'wake-up calls' are necessary in India not only for the dithering executive, but also for the slow-grinding judiciary. Experience, however, suggests that the temptation to snooze persists, even after the shrill ring of reality — the alarm itself serving as well as any guaranteed soporific" Again, Joseph Conrad was convinced that "It is not justice, the servant of men, but Accident, Hazard and Fortune — that ally of patient Time, that holds an even and a scrupulous balance."

The delay in delivering justice is bound to shake people's faith in judiciary, and to some extent it has denied justice to the people. Earlier, Home Minister L.K. Advani, at a conference at Ahmedabad on 'Legal Aid Orientation pointed out that effective provision of justice is the primary objective of the judicial process and this objective is frustrated by the inordinate delays in the disposal of cases. He has gone to the extent of saying that 'the judiciary instead of being a solution had itself become a problem'. Much time of the courts is wasted in "giving dates", and it creates a sense of deep anguish and frustration among clients. Many legal experts refer to a mandatory provision of the law which lays down that 'when a case is taken up in a court, it should be heard from day to day and that no adjournment should be given unless circumstances make this inescapable' and such circumstances must be recorded. Mr. H.D. Shourie elaborates the point by citing figures, ".....in the courts of U.P. where the number of pending civil cases is 9.25 lakh. Out of these about 3 lakh are one to three years old, about 2.5 lakh are three to ten years old, about 60,000 cases are over ten years old, possibly including those embroiling succeeding generations in litigations started by ancestors."[1]

To sum up in the words of Mr. V.M. Tarkunde, "Judicial delays constitute the most serious defect in the present judicial system in the country."[2] Such excessive judicial delays have marred the image of the judiciary; reasons whatever they may be, for delay, must be traced in order to reduce the number of pending cases. The Hindustan Times aptly remarks (Dec. 8, 1998)," Apart from the problem of the backlog of cases — over 30 million of them by the last count — the judicial system needed to put itself under the microscope and see why the judicial procedures had become so dilatory and justice was not reaching the needy .... The fact that like much else in our national life, the judiciary no longer commanded as much awe and respect as it used to in the years

1 Times of India - Clogged courts : Cases Backlog can be cleared; Aug. 12, 1998.

2 The Hindustan Times - Judicial Delays - July 2, 1998.

immediately after Independence should be of widespread concern."[1] Now the point needs no further elaboration!

However, the Chief Justice of India Dr. A.S. Anand has a new year resolution that he wants the subordinate judiciary to follow down the line. He wants the speedy clearance of a huge backlog of pending cases. Therefore, he has declared 1999 as an "Year of Action" for the judciairy and called for the quick disposal of old cases on the basis of the pendency period. Let us hope that the judiciary will come up to the people's expectation.

National Judicial Commission

Here, a discussion in fine about the National Judicial Commission will not be out of context since persons in many quarters of society have started raising their eyebrows at the credibility of the judiciary. As Home Minister L.K. Advani expressed his views, "There has been a considerable dent in the credibility of this important democratic institution." Besides, politicians and statesmen, persons of the world of law feel upset at the growing evils of corruption and nepotism in the judiciary. It is a matter of serious concern. Justice P.B. Sawant while addressing the High Court Bar Association, has expressed concern over the corruption in the judiciary and the trend of populism among certain judges in the garb of judicial activism. He said, "these two are very disturbing developments..... corruption was happening at some places at

1 Ibid, Dec. 8, 1998.

all levels and even if one or two judges were corrupt, it marred the image of the entire judiciary."[1] The other day former chief Justice of India, Justice J.S. Verma said that "Judges of the Supreme Court and the High Court should be brought under the ambit of a new law on the lines of the Prevention of Corruption Act to make them more accountable for their misconduct." He further added, "today the judges of the superior judiciary in India are not answerable to any one for their misconduct as neither impeachment procedures nor internal judicial machinery is workable."[2] The legal experts and other intellectuals stress the need to have a national judicial commission to nip the evil in the bud.

Attorney-General Soli J. Sorabjee has also supported the setting up of a national judicial commission which will look after the appointments and transfers of judges. He asserted that it was high time that a mechanism was devised to "discipline" the judges. The Attorney-General proposed that the commission should have five members — two supreme court judges, a high court chief justice, a "distinguished" retired supreme court judge and a lawyer from its Bar. He is firmly of the opinion that "Such a commission must inspire confidence and its credibility and independence are beyond doubt."[3] Similarly, President K.R. Narayanan expressed his desire that "all major regions and sections of the society should be represented in the judiciary along with the requirements of merit and high standards maintained by it."

1 The Hindustan Times; July 17, 1998.

2 Ibid, Aug. 9, 1998.

3 The Times of India, Dec. 7, 1998.

It is expected that such a commission will be able to monitor as well initiate moves for internal reforms regarding appointment and transfers of judges.

Such judicial commission is working smoothly in other countries such as Australia, New Zealand, Canada etc., and it has lent dignity to the judiciary. People look upon it with regard and faith. It has ever upheld credibility to the hilt. The commission will not only prove helpful to people but also to the judges who have grievances within the judiciary. The courts also have other problems like conditions of service and lack of proper infrastructure; it would help improve their conditions of service. Justice Rajindra Sachar is also suspicious of uprightness in the matter of appointment and transfer of judges and quotes the Supreme Court judgement about the possibility of fallibility in this matter.

"It cannot be denied that predisposition or subtle prejudice or unconscious prejudice or what in Indian language is called Sanskar are inarticulate major premises in the decision making process. That element in the decision making process cannot be denied, it should be taken note of."[1] Sometimes the judges find themselves in an embarrassing situation when they are transferred out of sheer prejudice or resentment. "We have honest and competent judges transferred while leaving undisturbed those of doubtful integrity. By all means, use all courses open to deal with judges against whom suspicion exists, but do not reduce the

1 An article "Need For Judicial Reform", The Hindustan Times, Dec. 22, 1998.

status of a High Court judge, who is constitutionally speaking as much of a bulwark and essential for the foundations of democracy as a Supreme Court Judge."[1]

However, the Chief Justice of India, Justice A.S. Anand, does not relish the idea of constituting a judicial commission. He does not think it a lofty idea but only an effort "to share the judicial cake." He has a valid point to oppose the commission : "Is it not too presumptuous to say that those who are outside the judiciary and are almost strangers to the judicial fraternity would be in a better position to participate in the selection of those who have to manage the administration of justice in the country?"[2]

Again, "I am unable to appreciate as to how those, whether from the executive or representing the legislature, who do not have any first-hand knowledge and information about the system and its man power, can be in a position to arrive at an objective decision"

In fact, Justice Anand has based his views on "The recent guidelines of a nine-judge bench of the Supreme court for wider consultations in the subject of appointment and transfer of judges which obviated the need for an independent judicial commission."[3] Justice Anand does not speak like a layman; he has a strong ground so his views cannot be brushed

1 Ibid.

2 The Times of India, Dec. 7, 1998.

3 The Hindustan Times, Dec. 8, 1998

aside at once. There should be a healthy discussion about the pros and cons of such a commission which may keep a tight rein on the judiciary. Independence of the judiciary must be preserved at all costs. Judiciary - ever bright - eyed and bushy - toiled!

Education a Shambles

That we have become a nuclear state, may be a matter of pride and prestige but it is a glaring truth that we are not an educated people even when the golden beams of the 21st Century - sun have begun to peep. In spite of the constitutional provision even after a full fifty years of independence, nearly half of our population is stuck in the mire of illiteracy. According to the UNICEF report "State of the World's Children 1999", India will be the largest country of illiterates. The parliamentary Committee headed by S.B.Chavan, was tabled in Parliament a day after the UNICEF's report and "its claims about the progress with the Universalization of Elementary Education (UEE) goals were found dubious. Though on paper, 94 per cent of the total population has a primary school within 1 km, and 83.98 per cent has an upper primary school within 3 km., the goals of planning have been missed by miles."

"At the end of the Eighth Plan period, 6.3 crore children in the 6-14 age group are still out of school. The vast majority of them are girls and children of Scheduled Castes and Tribes. The rate of drop-outs was envisaged to be controlled at 20 per cent for primary and 40 per cent for upper primary stages, but 34.5 per cent still drop out at the primary and 51.6 per cent at upper primary levels."*

* "According to NSS, most children drop out because of economic reasons. UNICEF says they end up as child labours - while lack of interest, the pressure of domestic chores on girls and, of course, gender discrimination, also contribute to the malaise. While UNICEF did not go into State-wise break-up, the parliamentary committee identified the five eastern States of Arunachal Pradesh, Bihar, Manipur, Sikkim and Tripura too have more than 60 per cent drop - outs. Mizoram and Orissa are in the second category (50-59 per cent) while seemingly progressive states like Andhra Pradesh, West Bengal, Karnataka and Gujrat have 40-49 per cent drop-outs. The committee found more children drop-out after class 5 than before it. And more girls than boys opt out. The worst performer is Bihar where 82.73 per cent of girls don't complete education. Most often, head masters of primary schools simply show all school eligible children in the village as "enrolled" and don't bother to find out how many are actually attending. On one of its State visit, the committee found cases of double enrolments."

The Hindustan Times, Dec. 14, 1998.

The committee confirmed UNICEF's remarks when it stated that students often sit on bare floors and in the vast majority of primary schools, two or three classes are conducted simultaneously by the same teacher. A deplorable plight indeed.

Let us have a look at the constitutional provision. Article 45 has clearly directed the State to ensure by 1960 "free and compulsory education for all children until they complete the age of fourteen years."This directive has obtained the status of the Fundamental Right of every citizen as per the Supreme Court judgement in the Unnikrishnan case (1993). Ironically enough, almost half of India's children and two-thirds of the girls are deprived of school education even today. Not to speak of education and nutritious food, they do not get a square meal and sufficient clothing. On the contrary, they are forced to do forbidden 'Child labour' in hazardous conditions when it is time to play and learn. In misery and misfortune they forget everything. They get no time to have a look even at a book of alphabets.

"A girl child (aged six) engaged in child labour can be envisaged as having been 'constitutionally educated' if she can be enrolled in a non-formal stream for three years and then in the National Literacy Mission's adult literacy programme for the next two years, without even having stepped into the village school."[1] The excerpt has drawn a clear picture of our education, our policy and our sincerity in our efforts. It needs no further comment.

The provision given in Article 45 of the Constitution can be marked with three distinct characteristics.

First : it is the only clause in the constitution that specifies a target date, i.e. 1960 for the achievement of the directive.

1 Excerpted from a document of Bharat Jan Vigyan Jatha, an all India Voluntary network of people's science groups.

Second : the reference to "the age of fourteen years" expresses a serious commitment to at least eight years of elementary education.

Third : the constitution, though vaguely, speaks of ensuring education and not only literacy. The word 'education' sounds more than literacy. It embraces both spiritual and worldly life. It makes man a citizen of a civilized world. Dr. S.Radhakrishnan has aptly defined it:

"If education is to help us to meet the moral challenge of the age and play its part in the life of the community, it should be liberating and life giving. It must give a basic meaning to personality and existence and equip us with the power to overcome spiritual inertia and foster spiritual sensitivity."[1] It was the real aim of the architects of the constitution behind using the word 'education'. Indeed, a noble and well - conceived aim.

No serious attempt has been made so far to educate the children of this country and the promise made in the constitution has proved a waste of words. "The recent systematic attempts as part of the World Bank agenda in India to dilute the nation's commitment from eight years of elementary education to five years of primary education a nd from education to literacy, therefore, blatantly violate the constitution. Ironically, several reputed voluntary

1 Radhakrishnan, S. True Knowledge, Orient Paper Backs, New Delhi; 1984, Preface.

organisations have colluded with the government from 1988 (the year the National Literacy Mission was inaugurated) onwards in watering down the constitutional commitment to UEE."[1]

I would like to focus the kind attention of the judiciary on the National Policy on Education (1986). It was the first policy document of the Government in post-independence India "Which unabashedly declared that the State would not provide school facilities to almost half of the nation's children (and two thirds of the girls). Instead, the policy asserted that those children who cannot get access to the primary school will be provided what was claimed to be its "equivalent through the non-formal stream."[2] A crystal clear and blatant dilution of the constitutional obligation on the Government's part.

In fact, the policy has set double standards in educational facilities for children who hail from different socio-economic sections of the society. The policy does not conform to Article 45 of the constitution and the government has directly or indirectly supported the so called "public schools and other private schools from the fifties onwards." That is why these private schools are flourishing like mushrooms in every town and village of the country. It is the common experience of the parents that most of these schools

1 An article by Anil Sadgopal - "A Fraud on our Children," The Hindustan Times; Dec. 20, 1998.

2 Ibid.

have turned into big shops. I personally know many persons who have become money bags due to their public school. Surprisingly, the Government issues them a No objection certificate (NOC).

"The 1986 policy further marginalised the mainstream government school system by setting parallel layers to it," says Mr.Anil Sadgopal, "This policy led to Navodaya Vidyalayas for the so-called "talented children" drawn from the better-off segments of rural society, and the cheap, ill-conceived non-formal centres for child labour."[1] Again — "It was amazing that policy makers could dare to conceive of providing a so-called educational "facility' that was designed to be even below the discredited government school while the per-child per-year cost (at 1990 prices) worked out to more than Rs.10,000 in Navodaya Vidyalaya and around Rs. 700/- in a typical government primary school the non-formal centre got away by spending a pittance of Rs.100."[2] Despite this fact, the Government claims that non-formal education is equivalent' to the formal school.

For this poor show all political parties are to blame since they have had opportunity to rule over different states but being busy in the power game they have bothered least to go through Article 45 of the constitution which aims at making children better citizens of tomorrow. They have, in fact, not given top priority to the education of children who are the promise of the future. Now they look despairingly into the bleak dark future. What the blazes!

1 Ibid.

2 Ibid.

I must say that illiteracy and poverty are the biggest crimes on earth. And their eradication is the most challenging task. Today what we need is political will. The judiciary can awake and strengthen this political will by directing the executive to fulfill the constitutional obligation. It is incumbent on the state and it must be urged to do it. Nothing is more necessary for self-esteem than an educated nation. If we are strong in will, "It is not too late to seek a newer world."

Now-a-days people look to the judiciary for the solution to every problem. They are quite hopeful that it will come to their rescue. In such conditions when other wings of the State—the legislature and the executive, are dormant, the judiciary, being the guardian of the constitution, will take necessary steps which should not be frowned upon as transgression into the estate of the executive. To quote Justice Anand, the judiciary has intervened in certain areas because of the people's perception that judicial intervention is perhaps the only feasible correctional remedy available. There is, therefore, no need to treat this exercise as an attempt by the judiciary to either clutch at jurisdiction or to usurp the function of any other organ of the State."[1]

Again, "with a view to seeing that the judicial activism does not become 'Judicial Adventurism' and lead a judge going in pursuit of his own notions of justice and beauty, ignoring the limits of laws, the bounds of his jurisdiction and the binding precedents, the use of self-restraint is considered

1 The Hindustan Times, Oct. 30, 1998

essential and necessary."[1] Thus, the judiciary is well aware of its limitations, it tries to relieve people within the constitutional limits without defying the sanctity of the constitution. It has to protect the public faith reposed in it. "Public resort to the court to suppress public mischief," says Justice Anand, "is a tribute to the Justice system ."

Last but not least, Justice Khanna's word of warning should be kept in mind : "It is also necessary for all sections of the society to bear in mind the warning that a society so riven that the spirit of moderation and discipline is gone, no court can save, that a society where that spirit flourishes, no court need save; that in a society which evades its responsibility by thrusting upon the courts the nurture of that society, that spirit in the need will perish."[2]

1 Ibid.

2 AIR; Dec. 1998 p. 201.

CHAPTER EIGHT

Judicial Activism - boon or bane

Boon

Judicial activism has more in it than meets the eye; it is the timely defence of the people's faith in the wisdom of the judiciary though triggered off by slugglishness and non-accountability of the other two organs of the Government. Their prolonged passivity has created a vacuum in the system and the judiciary by discharging its onerous duty it has not only filled the vacuum but also responded to the people's call. To quote Mr.Kuldip Nayar "Ideally, Parliament and the executive are the custodians of honest public life..... but when the custodians themselves compromise with corruption or politicise it, the judiciary has to step in. This is what has happened"[1]. The judiciary has done a great service to the nation by creating on abhorrence for the wrongs in public life. It should neither be misunderstood nor misinterpreted as all are free to think in their own ways. As Justice J.S. Verma opines "freedom of expression is not to be confused with a licence to make unfounded, unwarranted and irresponsible remarks against the judges of the courts."[2] Of course, its aim has been to "nudge, bestir and activate" the executive and legislature into a conscientious performance of their duties,

1 The Hindustan Times; Dec 17, 1996.

2 Ibid; March 30, 1997.

not to demoralise them. A corrupt person has always a guilty conscience which restrains him from taking things in their right perspective. The system which we had adopted with high hopes and aspirations, has been defeated due to its custodians and people's faith in the system therefore has been shattered. The former Prime Minister I.K. Gujral accepted openly, "the rampant corruption in different walks of life was undermining the faith and confidence of the people in democracy and administration".[1] He also came forth with the suggestion of setting up special courts "to try graft cases". Is there anything more shameful than the Prime Minister's open acceptance of corruption in public life ? Again he has pointed out, "corruption I say with regret and pain, has seeped into the veins of this nation. It is not only those who are in ministerial positions who are corrupt, of course, they are and something drastic has to be done about them."[2] The stunned, shocked and anguished Prime Minister goes on describing the horrendous situation, "Nothing works without pay-offs. Whether in a police station, the Patwari's office, the electricity department or the water department, they are fleecing people, especially those belonging to poorer and weaker sections. The common man is extremely hariassed and weary of corruption."[3] In such a situation the judiciary has rendered a great service to the nation. It has brought a ray of hope to the people that there is an institution which is fully aware of the people's troubles; and it can discharge its

1 Ibid; June 3, 1997.

2 Ibid; July 12, 1997.

3 Ibid; Aug 16, 1997.

duty conscientiously to relieve them. It is an effort to regard people's authority over that of the Government. It is an enlightened response to the call of the nation. Some critics have described judicial activism as "judicial transgression" when the court made it clear categorically that it had every right to pull up an officer for tardy investigation. In fact, it is not judicial transgression but a check upon political pressure on the officers as they hesitate to go against their political masters. It is the basic principle of the philosophy of justice that a fair and free probe must be ensured. This check is necessary to prevent the executive and legislature from getting arbitrary and wayward. If the court feels that some particular agency or officer is not working properly or is hesitant to probe into the case against his master, it becomes painfully indispensable for the court to pull up the particular officer or agency. If the investigating agencies remain uninfluenced by political masters, the courts will be able to do their work easily. For this harsh act, the courts are not to blame but endemic corruption in the form of political and bureaucratic nexus which is quite unexpected in a democratic system. The persons under suspicion make every possible effort to dodge the law. Corruption in this country has left not even an iota of shame or moral sense in the corrupt. They go on shifting charges on to other persons instead of confessing or making a public apology. They set no examples before the country but try to prove themselves virtuous. They seem to be the pyramid of all virtues. On the other hand the corrupt whether bureaucrats or politicians "walk majestically to the courts, dressed up as though they are to attend a wedding reception and acknowledged people's greetings as though court processes are a Nobel Prize citation."[1] The former Prime Minister I.K. Gujral himself feels helpless though he wants people to resist But the courts do not feel helpless; they are quite hopeful of doing something substantial at least to create an awareness among people. They will try to bring the culprits to book because no one is above the law.

Now the entire system is in bedlam. Persons of criminal records have entered the Parliament and have got ministerial berths. Their chief aim is to achieve power and use it for their own maximum benefit. During the debate on some national issue, the Parliament is no better than pandemonium. People all over the country are taken aback to see them wrangling with one another. The Lok Sabha speaker P.A. Sangma was so shocked at the behaviour of the M.P.s that he "threatened to resign if they did not listen to him". He asked painfully, "Is there any difference between Parliament and the Boat Club? Don't you feel sorry for converting the Parliament into a street I feel ashamed of being the speaker of such a House".[2] It is clear that they care least for the dignity and decorum of the Parliament. What is expected in the House an "excellent oratory and reasoned arguments" to arrive at some conclusion, has become a distant dream. A major part of an entire session goes in such wranglings which mar the dignity of the House. Such shocking incidents which include, "intemperate utterances and

1 The Hindustan Times; June 19, 1997.

2 Ibid; July 2, 1997.

even physical violence" have reasons behind them. Persons who are coming to the house are from criminal backgrounds. They have least regard for moral values or the ideals which the House stands for. They have no knowledge of the country's history, no pride of her heritage, no education with a decent language and no memory of the heroes of the struggle for freedom. Their top priority stands for power — only power. I have often wondered what a rude shock it must be to the faith of the people in the Parliament when certain proceedings are televised live to the nation. The tumultuous scenes and extra Parliamentary exercise in the legislature draw its hue and colour from the persons composing it. Of course, such persons can hardly be expected to maintain any standard of the House. In spite of having no political insight they have a great charm in politics which makes them feel above the law. With the help of political parties which first use them "to capture booths and win elections", these "law breakers" become "law makers" with no hesitation. Mr. Galbraith has aptly described it as "a functioning anarchy."

Now the matter has come to such a predicament that most of the people are of the opinion that the system which we adopted with high hopes, is on the verge of collapse. The entire system is just a waste land. The President K.R. Narayanan has rightly observed, "a social movement or a wide spread national movement is needed to cleanse the system."[1] He is very much doubtful of the stability of the system. Since doubt has crept into people's minds, they begin to think about

1 The Hindustan Times; Aug 15, 1997

the replacement of the system which may give political stability to the country. Political stability and a decent political culture is essential not only for maintaining law and justice but also speeding up the progress of the country. The Government comprising 13 parties, now 14, is dependent on outside support from two parties. Hence, instability, like the sword of Damocles, is hanging over the Government and the Prime Minister, I.K. Gujral in spite of his iron will to remove corruption is helpless. He can do nothing unless he gets a "magic wand". A clear reason lies behind his helplessness — his dependence on other parties. This position of helplessness is pitiable; it should not be prolonged.

What was happened in Bihar, has proved that democracy in India is nothing but a farce. It has far-reaching effects on public life. The Bihar Chief Minister, Mr. Laloo Prasad Yadav, has been described as the "worst type of politician in today's India." (H.T. July 31, 97) Bengal, too, has not lagged far behind Bihar in misusing public funds (4.29 crore rupees). Other states too are not free from this infectious disease. This bitter legacy should not be carried out further. Judiciary — only the judiciary can step in !

It is a matter of pride that our constitution "gave us a flying start and equipped us adequately to meet the challenges of the future. Unfortunately, over the years we dissipated every advantage we started with, like a compulsive gambler bent upon squandering an invaluable legacy".[1] Now the

1 Ibid;

nation's picture which has emerged after 50 years of independence, is dismal as well as hopeless. Corruption is the phenomenon of today's life. The malady of corruption has gone deep and is spreading fast and wide. Truly speaking things are getting worse day by day. The statement made by Chief Justice J.S. Verma shows the height of corrupt practices affecting adversely the system when he disclosed that "he and his brother judges (S.P. Barucha & S.C. Sen) on the hawala bench had come under persistent pressure not to hear the matter." (H.T. July 15, 97) Justice Verma observes again, "All types of things began happening to me and the same things are happening to my brother judges. We are getting all types of calls with the same persons persistently trying to reach us and influence us."[1] However, the 'gentleman' has managed to reach one of the brother judges (S.C. Sen) of the bench. Obviously Justice Sen is upset. After all, judges, too, are men of flesh and blood; sooner or later the 'cheap tactics' of the gentlemen may work. Whatsoever it may be, Justice Verma has made it clear in no uncertain terms, "These are very cheap tactics and they are not going to work".[2] Simultaneously, Justice Verma has categorically ruled out any change in the bench; surely it has strengthened the people's faith in the judiciary. Kudos to the judiciary!

The incident has made one thing clear that the 'gentleman' must have links with the game of power politics and must belong to the "high echelons of the political

1 Ibid; July 15, 1997.

2 Ibid.

hierarchy." It is definitely an interference in the process of justice; and it is dangerous for the system. It is really hard for the judges to work under "persistent pressure." Such "cheap tactics" must not be allowed to break in on the course of justice at any cost. Every effort of such brazen 'gentlemen' must be frustrated. It is the sacred duty of the Government to put down such nefarious attempts at "the highest citadel of justice." If the Government fails, people may rise for the cause. After all tolerance and magnanimity have their limits.

It is note-worthy that a section of the people in the country look at the judiciary with suspicion as superceding the executive and the legislature. They have made much hue and cry over the active role of the judiciary. They are in the quest of an opportunity to divest the judiciary of its power. They have plans "to bring forward bills to regulate judges' appointments and check public interest litigation". Such plans may be described as sinister since politicians are much scared to see the courts hauling up "senior politicians or government functionaries". Even the former Prime Minister I.K. Gujral has expressed his deep concern over the "misuse" of Public Interest Litigation. If such sinister plans are furthered, it will go against the constitution. The verdict of the seven-judge constitution bench of the apex court held that the parliament could not divest the apex court and the high courts of their power of judicial review even "by way of constitutional amendment." Referring to the various judgements of the apex court and the U.S. Supreme Court, Justice Ahmadi, who delivered the 89-page judgement on behalf of the court, ruled "that the power of judicial review vested in the high courts and the apex court empowering them to scrutinise legislative action was integral and an essential feature of the constitution." Again making it clear, Justice Ahmadi observes, "ordinarily, therefore, the power of the high court to test the constitutional validity of legislations can never be ousted or excluded."[1] Naturally, the verdict has come out of a clear sky for those who want to put a bridle on the judiciary. Briefly, to quote Mr. Bal Krishna, "Last but not the least, the judgement would go a long way in safeguarding the independence of the judiciary and protect the superior courts from any executive or legislative attempts to interfere with the making of their decisions."[2]

Moreover, such fear is baseless. Are our courts incapable of understanding the petitioner's intention? No, certainly not. The courts meant for "the poor and struggling masses of this country" should not be mistaken for their judicious decision. The courts understand well how to act in the interest of the people. If we want to put a restraint on the judiciary out of sheer baseless fear, it will be against the grain of democracy. As Chief Justice J.S. Verma has pointed out the PIL is "a correctional device" as well as a means "to ensure speedy dispensation of justice."

To all intents and purposes, the judiciary has ever been conscious of its modus operandi in which malignity

1 The Hindustan Times; March 24, 1997.

2 Ibid.

or prejudice has no room. No decision is irrevocable; there is ample scope for self-correction. This awareness can easily check the misuse of PIL. Two instances are in point. First, in the case of Mr.Kalpnath Rai, the apex court has shown its love and longing for justice by granting bail to him. (later he was acquitted). The apex court has not only granted him bail but also reprimanded the TADA court by pointing out "that Mr.Dhingra (TADA court judge) had not taken into account certain basic principles of criminal jurisprudence in arriving at conclusions about a dismissed officer of the Indian Police Service and about the role of the former minister in harbouring terriorists."[1] Secondly, the Patna High Court has punished two judicial officers — the Jamshedpur sub-judge Tabarakh Hussain and senior sub-judge N.P. Verma. "Hussain has been suspended while Verma has been demoted ....."[2] What Oliver Holmes said long ago, "the life of law has not been logic; it has been experience" is quite true of our judicial system. Both of the cases show the "process of self-correction in the judicial system." It is comprehensive and moderate. Ever in the interest of the nation.

In such a messy state the judiciary has come out like showers to relieve the people of scorching heat. Hence, in today's circumstances the judiciary can be nothing else but a boon.

1 Ibid; April 12, 1997.

2 Ibid; Aug 22, 1997.

Bane

On the other hand there is another school which does not hold the judiciary as sacred cow. The advocates of this school raise the question—who will judge the judges? Justice J.S. Verma seems to share the same views when he says, "These days we (judges) are telling everyone what they should do but who is to tell us?" They are of the opinion that the decisions of the courts need to be subjected to scrutiny like the other two organs of the government. It is not superior to them. It cannot supercede the executive and the legislature since India has a written constitution which clearly defines the scope of the three-the executive, the legislature and the judiciary. Hence, any sort of clash among them is unwarranted. Critics have expressed their deep concern over judicial activism in recent years. They firmly hold that the judiciary is over enthusiastic and is interfering in the work of the executive. "Unfortunately, this is precisely what the Supreme Court and the High Courts have been doing in a number of cases and a weak and pusillanimous Government has been surrendering in every case. The investigation of an offence may lead to a judicial process but provided the investigation is done according to law, the investigating agency is certainly within the supervisory control of the executive."[1] This may be called judicial authoritarianism. Its pulling up an investigating agency and taking supervisionary power in its own hands shows clearly the authoritative nature of judiciary. It hurts the executive. Again, "For the courts to order that the

1 The Hindustan Times; Feb 13, 1997.

Government will not exercise its power of supervision and direction under section 4 of the Police Act is an undue interference. For the Government to direct that before an investigation into a particular case is undertaken prior approval should be sought is perfectly valid, unless the law prohibits it. Nowhere in the world is the power of the police to investigate unfettered, except in a dictatorship, and the power to supervise, direct and control the police must vest in the executive. The courts may intervene only if the Government uses its power arbitrarily."[1] The modus operandi of the judiciary is increasing tension between it and the executive. It is an alarming sign for a democratic system. It impedes the smooth running of the system. It should be borne in mind that the collision of the judiciary and the executive may lead to disaster; so the former should try to avert any possible conflict, The Hindustan Times points out in its editorial (July 3, 97) "there are hints that the Government is not, too, pleased with the current phase of the so called judicial activism." That is why the Government has started thinking of putting restraints on the judiciary in some way or the other.

The critics opine that the judiciary is riding high and so in over-enthusiasm is trying to cross limits in the guise of judicial activism which is wholly unconstitutional as well as undemocratic. The long arm of the law is encroaching upon the Parliament. It has made the representatives suspicious about its judicial role. They find the judiciary growing somewhat dictatorial in its nature. The observation of the

1. Ibid.

Hindustan Times (Feb 21, 97) is worth quoting, "in the past three years the judiciary has systematically superseded the representative estates of democracy, Parliament and the Government — and may have stepped far beyond the role assigned to it under the constitution." Slamming the judiciary for its role The Hindustan Times writes further, "over the past 15 months the sway of the judiciary over areas that once belonged to Parliament and the Government has increased without much challenge. Politicians and bureaucrats have viewed with justified alarm the transformation of activist justice into judicial tyranny." It appears that the judiciary is bent upon showing up the shortcomings of political as well as bureaucratic institutions instead of dispensing justice speedily. The critics have attacked the judiciary for its dictatorial role which is posing danger for the other institutions of democracy. If this dictatorial temperament of the judiciary is allowed to go on, justice will be a cry in the wilderness. Hence, its tyrannical role should be curbed; it is quite alien to the democratic spirit. If it desires to do something worth-while, it must create a healthy atmosphere in which all the three institutions of the Government may flourish. To quote Mr.P.N. Duda, "The Supreme Court is the master of its own calendar. It can hear a case, refuse to hear it, initiate a matter for enquiry, give reasons for its orders or pass orders without reasons. With such massive range of powers over people and the other two wings of the Government, the only course available to the citizenry is debate, and initiation of appropriate proceedings against the judges."[1] The so called judicial activism has gone far beyond judicial review. It is likely to take administration in its own hands. Its traditional role of correcting the mistakes of the executive and the legislature has rippled away. It has assumed a new role of tyrannical activist whose concern is to demoralise the other wings of the Government Mr.Duda shares the people's fear and further adds, "It may interfere in anything which may have nothing to do with the justice according to laws. The courts lay down policies and enforce them, shelving the constitutional repositories of these powers in the backyard"[2]. In fact, this sort of immunity from any demand of accountability will make it more despotic than "despotism of politicians."

The absolute nature of the judiciary has been assailed; its decisions are a step towards judicial despotism which will mar people's faith in justice. Here, the judiciary behaves like an arrigant activist. Its power of punishing for contempt of court is an effective weapon to quiet the critics. The Apex Court has given certain decisions which have armoured the judges against any accounting. In this regard Justice Khanna says, "genuine criticism has to be accepted. Punishment under the contempt of court act is no answer to positive criticism."[3] Many people are of the opinion that something must be done

1 The Hindustan times; Jan 15, 1997.

2 Ibid.

3 Ibid; Jan 20, 1997.

to check it as the former union Law Minister puts it, "Bonafide statement of facts should not constitute contempt. Parliament should take up the matter and make the necessary constitutional amendment so that the contempt law is not used incessantly to save the dignity of an arrogant judge."[1] Speaking on the matter, Mr. Narayan says, "The contempt law is contemptible as it allows the same person to be the prosecutor as well as the judge. Also, it is wrong for the judges to think that they are not open to scrutiny. These days judges have started speaking outside their judgements in a manner (which is) derisive of the other pillars of democracy. This is disconcerting. I believe in freedom — even imperfect freedom rather than perfect justice."[2] The contempt law should be modified. It should certainly not be used to satisfy one's ego. The legal experts go ahead to prove that the contempt jurisdiction needs amendment for the sake of a free and fair discussion over the decisions of the court. They refer to the case of a former chairman of the Bar Council of India when "the apex court held that if any lawyer was arraigned before the Supreme Court in a case of contempt, he can be given a token punishment provided for it but removed from the roll of lawyers for the rest of his life."[3] After this fateful decision the judges stand in a 'safe pill box' while the lawyers are in 'the dog-house'. It has created an embarrassing situation for the persons willing to join this profession. This is a sort of the highest immunity of judges. If a person talks

1 Ibid.

2 Ibid; Jan 15, 1997.

3 Ibid.

about the possibility of corruption in the courts, he will be punished. The case of Mr.Bal Thackeray who, in one of his articles, disclosed the wish of a judge (without name) for taking hush money in some case, proves the point when he was held guilty for contempt of court. Similarly, a professor of English in the Punjab University was sentenced for 'six months' for contempt of court. His only fault was that he criticised the judgement of the supreme court. Seeing this absolute power of the courts, no official or person will think of doing anything which may annoy the judiciary. In fact, "the test of quality of any system," as an American Supreme Court Judge, Oliver Wendell Holmes observes, "is to assess it on the hypothesis that its exercises falls in the hands of a bad man and asking whether the power can be abused?"[1]

Again the Patna High Court's remark has stirred up a hornets' nest when it claimed to have constitutional right to advise the President for the invocation of Article 356. Rajya Sabha members expressed deep concern over the court's remark. They questioned the court's jurisdiction in passing such a remark. The deputy leader of the Rashtriya Janta Dal Mr. Sompal said that the Patna High Court had "out stepped its jurisdiction in recommending President's rule in Bihar". Mr. Naresh yadav (J.D.) added that the court's observation was outside its jurisdiction. Mr.Jalaluddin Ansari (CPI) brushed aside the court's remark by saying that the House should not waste its time on the court's observation. Mr. Hansraj Bhardwaj (Cong.) former Minister of state for

1 The Hindustan times; Jan 15, 1997

law and justice felt a need for one all-party meeting on the broader issue of judicial jurisdiction. However, the House was divided in its opinion for a simple political reason but the court's observation is a red rag to the critics. To them it is some kind of a Murphy's law. "If the judiciary sees a chance to grab executive power, it will."[1] It is commonly known that the power of imposing President's rule vests with the President to be guided by the Governor or if the President is satisfied that there is a breakdown of constitutional machinery in a state. The courts have the power to decide the legality of the President's rule. Commenting on the court's observation The Hindustan Times writes in its editorial (Aug. 14, 1970), "the intervention of the judiciary at any stage other than that will not only be contrary to the spirit of the constitution but also amounts to violating the basic democratic concept of separation of powers as enshrined in the constitution." Again, the judiciary's inclination to authoritarianism is noticed when the Patna High Court, not long ago, suggested as an obiter dictum that the CBI should "ask for the army's help to effect the arrest of Mr. Laloo Prasad Yadav." (Later on the apex court condemned the advice of P.H.C.) Besides, the judges of the various courts have been seen indulging in this sort of practice. Such orders are seldom a part of their judgement. Most of the legal experts do not favour such acts of the courts. They believe that "rule of law is vastly different from rule by courts." They are led to believe that "the judiciary had arrogated to itself powers

1 Ibid; Aug 14, 1997.

of both the executive and the legislature."[1] Furthermore, citing the examples of "judicial transgression", the legal experts hold that "directing an officer not to report to his senior is taking activism too far." Indeed it has left the legal experts panic-stricken.

The judiciary has been found again lacking in reason in imposing damages amounting to Rs. 50 lakh on the former Petroleum Minister Satish Sharma* and Rs. 60 Lakh on the former Urban Development Minister Sheela Kaul. A senior Supreme Court lawyer Mr. P.P. Rao says in this connection, "Without giving a finding that the ministers were corrupt, the court should not have imposed exemplary damages on them. Before passing the orders, the court should have asked the Income Tax authorities or any competent authority to make a valuation of their assets."[2] The legal experts who have found the judgement arbitrary, are of the opinion that the courts must not usurp the discretion of the public authority which the Parliament has conferred on it. "An action of a minister

* *Allowing Mr. Sharma's petition seeking a review of the 1996 order, a three judge bench headed by Justice S. Saghir Ahmad said, " We are of the opinion that no case was made out against the petitioner." It said the earliest directions completely negated the law laid down by the Apex Court on several occasions. The bench observed that the case had been decided on peculiar facts, where the directions for exemplary damages and a CBI probe couldn't be sustained.*

The Apex Court directed the Govt. to refund the fine amount already deposited in the Govt. exchequer by Mr. Sharma.

1 Ibid; Jan 20, 1997.

2 Ibid.

cannot be held to be unreasonable merely because the court thinks it to be unreasonable"* argues one of the critics. The judiciary should first convince itself whether the concept of discretionary quota "does not offend the principles of equity and justice." There are several judges, too, who have been beneficiaries of discretionary quota.

The Delhi High Court raises its guard and defines 'discretionary quota' well in its judgement. The bench comrprising Mr. Justice Y.K. Sabharwal and Mr. Justice D.K. Jain stated at length, "Discretion implies good faith in discharging public duties. The exercise of discretion was to be based on relevant considerations." Analysing the question of discretion further the judges held, "When discretion is exercised by taking in extraneous considerations, it has to be quashed. The concept of absolute, untrampled or unfettered 'discretion' is wholly inappropriate to a public authority." The judgement further clarified "The concept of unfettered discretion is appropriate only when dealing with a private property and not when dealing with public property." Again the judges state, "The power is to use the 'discretion' and not to abuse it. The authority granted discretions has to exercise power in a fiduciary capacity. If the court finds that there were illegitimate motives in exercise of the 'discretion' that action would not be sustained."

The judges made it clear that they were in no way going to usurp the discretion of the public authority. "If the decision to make discretionary allotment is within the confines of reasonableness, the court will not go into the merits, even if two views are possible." Times of India (Sept. 4, 97) p. 3.

If the judiciary puts a restraint on the discretionary power of the public servant and a minister cannot use his discretion, it is no power at all. If a minister is expected to work with his power judiciously, he should be given guidelines. The Hindustan Times (Sept. 1, 1997) commenting on the Delhi High Court judgement writes, "The court may have been correct in its conclusion but the very nature of discretion allows a certain amount of whimsicality and arbitrariness. Once the principle of ministerial discretion is allowed under the law, the use of such discretion cannot be held illegal. It is irrelevant whether there is a "pattern of favouritism" in the allotment or the process is without any pattern at all."* The judgement breaks in the executive. It is the absolute nature of the judiciary which has got off the ground without much challenge. The judgement is opposed, "With the question whether a particular policy is wise or foolish, the court is not concerned; it can only interfere if, to persue it, is beyond the powers of the authority."

It is surprising to note that The Hindustan times in one editorial (April 26, 1997) stands by the judgement of the court and condemns the way in which the allotments of petrol pumps and LGP gas have been made from 'discretionary' quota by saying that "discretionary quota has become aberration which was not its original intention. It was meant to help the needy....." On the other hand in another editorial (sept. 1, 97) criticises the courts judgement and allows the abuse of discretionary quota by saying" ..... the very nature of discretion allows a certain amount of whimsicality or arbitrariness." What does it mean? Does it believe in criticism for criticism's sake ? However its stand does not stand to reason.

Further, the judiciary has been criticised on psychological grounds. Judges are after all human beings; they have all human weaknesses. They are prone to influence or temptation to do favours. Lok Sabha speaker P.A. Sangma points out this inherent flaw, "I have said this often and I repeat, judges are men of flesh and blood. At times, they have been influenced by the media blitz on certain issues. There has been a tendancy to take recourse to what has been said in a casual manner. This trend certainly smacks of judicial populism."[1] People have to suffer if the judgement has to be pronounced under the influence of media, money or mafia blitz. They have to take recourse to expensive and time consuming appeals for a review of these judgements. It would be a mistake to think that judges are demi gods. They have their own whims and inclinations which affect their decisions. They may bear an influence of some party ideology or religion in their minds while making decisions since they live in and through society. Actually, what is questioned, is their infallibility under some psychological inclination, not their integrity and probity. When there is much cry over rampant corruption in every walk of life, it is but natural for people to think of corruption even in the judiciary. They argue that if the two other wings of government can do wrong, how can the judiciary be infallible? It is a common question among people.

The judges see an erosion of moral values all around. They are vexed at the things shaping in society. They cannot remain unaffected. Hence, they have started speaking outside

1. The Hindustan Times; March 9, 1997.

their judgement which gives an idea of what is going on in their psyche. It is horrible to think that, "if the lower courts go wrong, one can approach the High Court and the Supreme Court. But heavens forbid if the Supreme Court goes wrong as to err is but human."[1]

Last but not the least, the critics are not happy with the style judiciary is assuming in the role of both the executive and the legislature. It is the path which leads to power. If it goes on unabated, it would be perilous for the entire system since the dictum goes, "Power corrupts and absolute power corrupts absolutely."

A Critique

In the present circumstances, the role played by the judiciary speaks for itself. Undoubtedly, the judiciary has kept its word made in the constitution. When the other two wings of the Government are off the rails, it is the judiciary which has stood its ground. It has read the pulse of the nation and responded to its call. When both the executive and the legislature are busy and have no time for those who have entrusted themselves, the judiciary has time and has come out to solace the hopeless hearts and to succour the faltering feet. Today when politicians and bureaucrats are playing fast and loose and people are suffering, the judiciary, worth its name, cannot sit silently. It is doing what it ought to do.

1. The Hindustan Times; Jan. 20, 1997.

Just one word for the critics' apprehension of superseding the executive and the legislature,. If the other two wings of the Government (as fairly expected) discharge their duty conscientiously and honestly, the judiciary is judicious enough not to interfere in their work. Justice Verma is firmly of the opinion, "We are not required to be told by anyone as to what we should do and we must have the moral authority to be able to tell others and expect them to behave in the manner in which we tell them to behave."[1] In fact, judicial activism has not degenerated into judicial despotism so far and one hopes that the court will go not so far as to be branded as judicial autocrat. Last but not least, the maxim goes without saying — Quis custodiet ipsos custodes — who shall judge the judge? Judges alone can judge themselves.

1 Ibid; Nov. 17, 1997.

Epilogue

We alone are responsible for the present precarious predicament we are witnessing all around. All of us have contributed to it in some way or the other. We should look at ourselves and accept the fact instead of shifting the blame on one another. During fifty years of independence whatever we have done, must be scrutinised carefully to arrive at some logical conclusion. The maelstrom around is a reflection of our thinking, our deeds and our life style. If we find ourselves surrounded by a myriad problems, we have to ask ourselves - who has created them? If our executive legislature or judiciary is corrupt, we are to blame. If our system has failed, it is our failure. If secessionist forces are at work, we have encouraged them. Surely, something has gone wrong with us. We are in the grip of false pride and prejudices. We have undermined national thinking due to our preference for petty ends. To quote N.A. Palkhivala, "We have too much government and too little administration; too many public servants and too little welfare; too many laws and too little justice. Consequently, no one knows who runs the country; it runs itself. We all are running with it." In fact, what we need today is a drastic change into the things, not on the surface of the things. Hence, introspection as well as confession must be our theme.

Today we are passing through a crisis thar demands

action instead of debate. We can neither leave it on the judiciary or any other wing of the government nor on fate and chance. Since we have a major share in the present thorny harvest no one can come to our rescue. It is we who have to pay for it. We can all avert the tragedy that is likely to befallus. Nothing is wrong with the system we have adopted; the fault lies within us, not in our stars. We have to take the plunge without care for our petty gains, to drive out every force which has held us back. Let high morals and uprightness be our source of energy. Since "if the moral fibre of the people is undermined by the corruption and opportunism, no institutional change, however, radical, will save the polity from crisis breakdown." Of course, the solution to all problems lies within us. It hardly matters if we do not have elaborate living standards provided we have a standard of life. What actually matters is commitment to goals with honesty and sincerity. Sacrifice is the cornerstone of great achievement. Words and deeds must match. An individual irrespective of race, colour or caste is the basis of grand success. Hence, an honest, upright and conscientious person has ever been an asset to the nation.

Besides an individual, we are a nation. What kind of nation are we or down aspire to be? We are to decide it. We have to keep pace with time; if we fail in setting the pace, we shall be left "to languish in the dustbin of history." The bare fact is-we have failed in all walks of life. Japan in Asia and West Germany in Europe were decades behind us in 1947;

and now they are a century ahead of us. We live in the euphoria of being the largest democracy in the world. While the fact is that "democracy has been converted into mobocracy and demagogy. Issues are not settled in the Parliament and legislatures, or court room or academic councils. These are settled on the street by the use of force." Is this the modus operandi of a democratic system? Is this the democracy we boast of? All democratic institutions—legislature, executive, judiciary, bureaucracy and seats of learning—are in shambles. After independence, we have failed in evolving a national culture in which all individual as well as sectional ideologies fade away. The idea of an independent nationhood of its own kind with our cultural values and eternal message envisioned by persons like Gandhi, Tagore etc. is eroding gradually. It has gone into oblivion. Now the phrases which used to churn the blood of even an ordinary person, have lost vigour and vitality; they only languish in the memory lane of the freedom fighters while they are at the fag end of their life. We have not succeeded in bringing about new culture with its roots in Indian soil. Neither have we parted with the past nor have we held to a westernized present. Consequently, double standards have prevailed which has encouraged sectional institutions in society and "this process of institutional difference followed a different trajectory in India". In the absence of the idea of nationhood with an undefined heritage, the movement headed by mighty leaders during the struggle for freedom became a party after independence which captured power and continued on the throne for more than four decades. No attention was paid to the simmering differences underneath; and later on they burst out as secessionist forces which have posed a great threat to the nation's integrity and solidarity. After independence all institutions and organizations have flourished without national ethos and an ideal moral culture. There is no co-ordination between two institutions; are feeling a sense of uneasiness within. They are victims of disparagement and disorientation. They are frowned upon for maladroitness. A civil society is still a distant dream. In a pluralistic society like ours there should be an institutional sense to ensure justice and equality. Contrary to it, the composite character of our society has created many intractable problems which are pulling down the democratic edifice brick by brick. The problem arose because the past 50 years have not been given a serious thought due to the lack of a national character; and they haunt every thinking mind like a ghost.

We have to rise above individualism to rekindle a national ethos to bring our country forward on the international globe as a powerful nation. It is high time to light the lamp of national awakening.

Diagnosis of the Present Syndrome

If the former Prime Minister I.K. Gujral's observation "Corruption has seeped into the veins of nation", is taken for granted, it is certain that the malady has gone deep down with the proliferation which is tearing body limb from limb. In such dismal conditions simple antibiotic or therapy does not work; something drastic need to be done— a massive operation to check proliferation. It is likely that some rotten organ has to be amputated. No matter if it happens for the sake of the rest of the body. It is both a painful and difficult task but it has to be done. So, a well - qualified amputator is needed. If we turn our back on the situation and the operation is not performed in time, the condition will be out of control. The former president R. Venkatraman has rightly assessed the situation, "That a revolution is preferable to this wretched system". 0f course the system has proved a total failure. So a 'total revolution' is today's imperative need. If we hang back in taking the intitiative to bring about radical changes, people will take the matter into their hand, and they will decide it on the street.

Sqn Ldr S.D.Mitro (Rtd.).

Writes a letter to the Hindustan Times (Sept 5, 1997)...............we seem to have become a nation of nincompoops and slaves at the hands of Government machinery, the law enforcement authority or even the judiciary : all of which, if not actually, at least appear tainted..............Politicians and bureaucrats, who are increasing in number apear to be indulging in a mass - scale rape of their country. The time has come for a few right thinking persons to re-organize and re-activate "Azad Hind Fauj" to fight the enemy within for the sake of fulinegenerations". In point of fact, this letter gives an idea of the people's mind. It shows the terms in which they have started thinking. Certainly, In this great fight people may be divided in their aims — but everyone will have his share in it. Some may be fighting for bread, while others for human values. Some may rise for justice and equality others for the nation's dignity. Those who will take arms to satisfy their belly, may be persuaded to give up the cause with the assurance of bread but those who fight for the values and dignity of life, will fight to the last. They will fight at the risk of their life. But resurrection is assured.

Corruption breeds demoralization; demoralization cowardice and cowardice fear. The corrupt are spineless and gripped with fear. They may be anxious to know the colour of the rvolution-my answer to them is "Red".

Bibliography

Articles

Aggarwal U.C. — 'Crusader Without Sword', The Hindustan Times, April 16, 1997

Agreste, John — The Limits of Judicial Supremacy: A Proposal for "Checked Activism", 14 Gn L. Rev. 1980

Ahmadi, A.M. — "Judicial Process : Social Legitimacy and Insitutional Viability" (1996) 4SSC (Jnl)1. Judicial Activism The Indian Advocate P 39

Bal Krishna — (i) 'Have Discretion, will pay fine', The Hindustan Times
(ii) 'Of, By and For Criminals?' The Hindustan times, Aug 31, 1997
(iii) 'Judiciary should Evolve Norms on Judges' conduct', The Hindustan Times, Oct. 20, 1997
(iv) 'Between Activism and Restraint', The Hindustan Times, March 10, 1997

Bahuguna, S.L. 'Culture of Harmony', The Hindustan Times, July 1, 1997

Bhatnagar, R. 'PIL: The Flip Side, The Times of India, Aug 12, 1997

Bhat K.N. 'Judges' Appointment: A stitch in Time Could Have Saved Nine; The Times of India, Aug 15, 1998

Bhatt, D.K. Judicial Activism Through Public Interest Litigation, The Indian Experience : AIR sc 1998

Bhat, U.L. "Exclusion of Jurisdiction under the Kerala Land Reforms Act: A Comment", 2Ac L.R. 339 (1978)

Bhargav, G.S. (i) 'Winners and Losers', The Hindustan Times, Mar 18, 1998
(ii) 'Checks and Balances', The Hindustan Times, Feb 13, 1997

Balckshield "Fundamental Rights and the Institutional Viability of Indian Supreme Court", 8 J.I.L.I. 139, 1996

Buch, M.N. — 'An Excess of Eithics', The Hindustan Times, May 13, 1997

Chidambaram, P. — 'Public Interest Litigation: Understanding a Concept', The Hindu, Jan 11, 1983

Chaudhary, N. — 'Long Arm of the Law will Finally Take its Course', The Times of India; Oct 7, 1996

Chaudhary — "The Golak Nath Case : A Critical Appraisal AIR 1968 (Jnl)

Das, J.K. — 'Lesiglators Are Not Sacred Cows', The Indian Express, Dec 16, 1996

Duda, P.N. — (i) 'A Matter of Balance', The Hindustan Times, Jan 15, 1997
(ii) 'Anatomy of Corruption', The Hindustan Times, Jan 19, 1997

Dahl, Robert A. — Decision Making in a Democracy, The Supreme Court as a National Policy Maker, 6 Journal of Public Law, (1957)

Davies, Edmond — "Judicial Activism". C.L.P.I. (1975)

Earl Latham — The Supreme Court as a Political Institution, Minnesota Law Rev., (1947)

Hardev Singh — 'Public Interest Litigation - Illusion and Reality', Popular Jurist; Jan-Feb 1984

Hegde, K.S. — Directive Principles of State Policy in the Constitution of India, (1971) S.C.J. (jnl)

Hingorani, N.H. — (i) Judicial Activism - I No Spirit of Confrontation, The Statesman; Jan 1, 1997
(ii) Judicial Activism - II Mission of Power By Executive, The Statesman, Jan 1, 1997

Jain, M.P. — Judicial Response to Privative Clauses in India, J.I.L.I. (1980)

Khanna, H.R. — (i) Role of the Judges (1979) I.S.C.C. (Jnl)
(ii) Judicial Activism, Politics India

Kasyap, S.C. — 'Selection of Judges', The Hindustan Times, Jul 2, 1998

Kaul, Sumer	'Few Blessings to Count', The Hindustan Times, Aug 1, 1997; 'The Fountain head', The Hindustan Times, Aug 22, 1997
Kothari, Rajni	'Democracy Beyond Parties', The Hindustan Times, Feb 12, 1998
Lal, Hardwari	'Separation of Powers', The Hindustan Times, Oct 17, 1996
Mahajan, Krishna	(i) 'Judging the Definition of Judges', The Indian Express, Mar 18, 1998 (ii) 'Ahmadi Must Protect Office of Public Prosecutor', The Indian Express, Oct 7, 1996 (iii) 'Is It Judicial Populism V Legal Discipline', The Hindustan Times.
Mohapatra, Satyen	'A Question of Precedence', The Hindustan Times, April 20, 1998
Mohan, Jag	'Supreme Court As Town Planner', The Indian Express, Dec 16, 1996
Mishra, Shyam	Nandan 'Influencing Judges', The Hindustan Times, July 30, 1997

Madhava, Mohan N.R. Public Interest Litigation, A Major Breakthrough in the Delivery of Social Justice, 9 J.B.C.I. (1982)

Mindelson, Wallace 'The Politics of Judicial Activism', Emory Law Journal (1975)

Nayar, Kuldeep (i) 'Defending Judicial Activism', The Hindustan Times, Dec 13, 1996
(ii) 'Pressure on Judges', The Hindustan Times, July 19, 1997
(iii) 'An Agenda For India', The Hindustan Times, Sept 13, 1997
(iv) 'Police and Human Rights', The Hindustan Times, June 7, 1997

Nandita Haksar 'Giving Justice Reach', The Indian Express (Cochin) Feb 9, 1984

Narsimhan, V.K. 'A suitable System', The Hindustan Times, May 2, 1997

Noorani, A.G. 'Judicial Activism V. Judicial Restraint', Span, Apr/May, 1997

Parmanand Singh Vindicating Public Interest Through Judicial Process; Emerging Trends and Issues, J.B.C.I; 1983

Pathak, Bindheswar	'It's Right, My Lord', The Hindustan Times, Apr 28, 1996
Patra, Prakash	'The Case for a Judicial Commission', The Hindustan Times, July 27, 1998
Rao, P.P.	'Pillar That Holds Basic Structure', The Hindustan Times, Mar 31, 1997
Raina, Jay	'Role of the Governor', The Hindustan Times, Apr 27, 1998
Rajeshwar, T.V.	'Distortions of Democracy', The Hindustan Times, Sept 17, 1997
Rustamji, K.F.	(i) 'Failure of the Police', The Hindustan Times, Apr 28, 1997 (ii) 'The Collapse of Justice', The Hindustan Times, Jan 28, 1998
S.B. Jaisinghani	'It's Judicial Asset', The Indian Express, Dec 23, 1996
Sachar, Rajendra	'Opportunity Missed to End Phone Tapping', The Hindustan Times,
Sachar, Rajendara	(i) 'Instrument of Change', The Hindustan Times, Jun 10, 1997

(ii) 'Appointment of Judges', The Hindustan Times, Mar 10, 1997

Singh, Amrik 'Judicial Activism', The Hindustan Times, Oct 19, 1996

Shenoy, T.V.R. 'The Judiciary Treading a Dangerous Path', The Hindustan Times, Sep 29, 1996

Shourie, H.D. 'Clogged Courts: Cases Backlog Can be cleared', the Times of India, Aug 12, 1998

Sayad, Liaquat Ali 'Balancing 'Absolutism' With Concensus', The Hindustan Times, July 27, 1998

Singh, Joginder 'Human Rights Violations by the Police', The Hindustan Times, Apr 27, 1998

Sarkar, Sumit 'Importance of Being Free', The Hindustan Times, Aug 19, 1997

Sodhi, S.S. 'Too much Serecy in Judicial Appointment', The Hindustan Times, Feb 13, 1997

Tarkunde, V.M. 'A Case For Timely Disposal', The Hindustan Times, July 27, 1998

Verma, J.S. 'Democracy without choice', the Indian Express, Mar 10, 1998

Willing, Richard 'U.S. Debate On Judicial Activism', The Times of India, Mar 17, 1997

Editorials, Interviews and Reports:

Editorials

Activism Again The Hindustan Times, Aug 21, 1998

Abuse of PIL The Hindustan Times, July 12, 1998

After Bihar, Bengal The Hindustan Times, July 11, 1997

A Juge Judged The Hindustan Times, April 12, 1997

A hornet's nest The Hindustan Times, Aug 14, 1997

A Sham Verdict The Hindustan Times, March 15, 1998

A Vote to Govern The Hindustan Times, March 30, 1998

A Wrong Undone The Hindustan Times, Feb 24, 1998

Back to Executive	The Hindustan Times, July 3, 1997
Bitter Legacy	The Hindustan Times, July 31, 1997
Bribe as half Crime	The Hindustan Times, April 20, 1997
Deplorable Conducts	The Hindustan Times, April 26, 1997
Heed the President	The Hindustan Times, Feb 26, 1998
High Life in Jail	The Hindustan Times, July 1, 1997
House in disorder	The Hindustan Times, July 24, 1998
In House Criminals	The Hindustan Times, Aug 22, 1997
Indiscreet, Indeed	The Hindustan Times, Sept 1, 1997
Judges' Case again	The Hindustan Times, July 29, 1998
Judging Judges	The Hindustan Times, Sept 13, 1997
Lacking Conviction	The Hindustan Times, Aug 30, 1997
Line up in Bihar	The Hindustan Times, July 30, 1997
Lest Ye Be Judged	The Hindustan Times, Feb 21, 1997

Mockery in Bihar	The Hindustan Times, July 28, 1997
Name the Offender	The Hindustan Times, July 16, 1997
One Nook less	The Hindustan Times, June 6, 1997
Out of Turn, Indeed	The Hindustan Times, June 23, 1997
Probing the scam	The Hindustan Times, Sept 1, 1997
Sangma's Anguish	The Hindustan Times, July 25, 1997
Sense and Secularism	The Hindustan Times, April 22, 1998
System in the Dock	The Hindustan Times, Sept 15, 1997
Thank You, Justice Verma	The Indian Express, Jan 23, 1998
Taking Law For a Ride	The Hindustan Times, July 24, 1998
Time to bury it	The Hindustan Times, March 4, 1998
The Helpless PM	The Hindustan Times, July 22, 1997
Turbulent Waters	The Hindustan Times, July 23, 1998
Words, Words, Words	The Hindustan Times.

Interviews :

Judicial Activism has ushered in hope : an interview of Justice J.S. Verma with the Indian Express, Jan 23, 1998

Judges can get influenced by the media blitz : an interview of P.Sangma with K. Srinivasan, The Hindustan Times, March 9, 1997

In a democracy, the big leap is for Parliament to take, not Judiciary : an interview of Justice Michael Kirby, Judge of the High Court of Australia, with Mr. Saloni Meghani, The Times of India,

Reports

1. A Judge who's keen to judge himself - Bal Krishna, The Hindustan Times, March 30, 1997

2. A Question of Precedence - Satyam Mohapatra, The Hindustan Times, April 20, 1998

3. CJ is the head of high court : SC, The Hindustan Times, Dec 4, 1997

4. CJ's tenure should at least 2 years - J.S. Verma, The Hindustan Times, Aug 29, 1998

5. Experts on Bihar : Nonsense on slits ...., mockery of democracy, The Hindustan Times, July 28, 1998

6. EC's directive raises points of order, The Hindustan Times, Sept 1, 1997

7. Fodder Scam Probe, The Hindustan Times, July 2, 1997

8. Four Guideposts to Judicial Activism - Justice Michael Kirby, The Hindustan Times, May 16, 1997

9. H.C. Can't Substitute its wisdom : Sc, Thc Hindustan Times, Sept 15, 1997

10. I've no magic wand to stop graft, The Hindustan Times, July 21, 1997

11. Judiciary should evolve norms on judges' conduct - Bal Krishna, The Hindustan Times, Oct 20, 1997

12. Justify people's faith, Verma exhorts judges, The Hindustan Times, Nov 17, 1997

13. Parliament cannot divest courts of their power - Bal Kishna, The Hindustan Times, March 24, 1997

14. Patna H.C. punishes judicial officers, The Hindustan Times, Aug 22, 1997

15. Political will Missing to Fight Corruption, The Hindustan Times, Nov 17, 1997

16. R.S. concern over Patna HC remarks, The Hindustan Times, July 14, 1997

17. Samant's concern over Corruption in Judiciary, The Hindustan Times, July 17, 1998

18. SC not stretching its role, CJ; The Hindustan Times, March 16, 1998

19. SC Clean Chit to Advani, Shukala in Hawala case, The Hindustan Times, March 3, 1998

20. Squandered legacy, The Hindustan Times, Aug 15, 1997

21. Who can Judge the Judges, The Hindustan Times, Jan 20, 1997

Authors	**Books**
Aggarwala, S.K.	*Public Interest Litigation in India: A Critique (1985)*
Andhyarujina, T.K.	*Judicial Activism and Constitutional Democracy in India (1992)*

Baxi, Upendra	*The Indian Supreme Court and Politics (1980)*
Basu, D.D.	*Introduction to the Constitution of India (1994)*
Cardozo	*The Nature of The Judicial Process*
Dhawan, Sudarshan & Khurshid (ed.)	*Judges and the Judicial Power (1985)*
Gupta, D.C.	*Indian government & Politics (1970)*
Iyer, Krishna VR	*Social Justice — sunset or down, 1993* *Law, Freedom and change,* 1975
Larry Collins & Dominique Hapierre	*Freedom at Midnight,* 1976
Micheal Edwardes	*The last years of British India,* 1967
Seervai, H.M.	*The Position of the Judiciary under the constitution of India,* 1970

Sidney, Hook *The Paradoxes of Freedom,* 1966

Vijay K. Gupta *Decision-making in the Supreme Court of India,* 1995

Cases :

1. Bar Council of Maharashtra V. M.V. Dabholor, AIR 1975 SC 2092

2. Bandhan Mukti Morcha V. Union of India, AIR 1984 SC 80 2

3. Dr. B.L. Wadhera V. Union of India, AIR 1996 SC 2969

4. Common Cause V. Union of India, AIR 1997 SC 1886

5. Chhetriya Pradushan Mukti Sangharsh V. State of U.P. AIR 1990 SC 2060

6. D.K. Basu V. State of West Bengal, AIR 1997 SC 610

7. Francis Coralie V. Administration, Union Territory of Delhi, AIR 1981 Sc 746

8. Hussainara Khatoon	V.	State of Bihar, AIR 1979 SC 1739
9. Indian Council for Enviro - Legal Action	V.	Union of India (1996)5 SCC221
10. J.P. Unnikrishnan	V.	State of Andhra Pradesh AIR 1993 SC 2178
11. Janta Dal	V.	H.S. Chaudhary, AIR 1993 SC892
12. Krishna Iyer	V.	R.A. Randon Misculany Legal and Other (1984)
13. K.M. Natraj	V.	State of Karnataka, AIR 1997
14. L.Chandra Kumar	V.	Union of India AIR 1997 SC 1125
15. Mumbai Kamgar Sabha	V.	Abdulbhai, AIR 1976 SC 1455
16. M.C. Mehatha	V.	Union of India, AIR 1987 SC 1086

17. M.C. Mehatha	V.	Kamalnath (1997)1 SCC 388
18. Mohd. Aslam	V.	Union of India (1994)2 SCC 48
19. Mechineni Krishna Rao	V.	Union of India, AIR 1997 Andhra Pradesh 275
20. Public Union for Democratic Rights	V.	Union of India, AIR 1982 SC 1473
21. P. Nalla Thampi	V.	Union of India, AIR 1985 SC 1133
22. Parmanand Kataria	V.	Union of India, AIR 1989 SC 2039
23. Peoples' Union of Civil Liberties	V.	Union of India, AIR 1997 SC 568
24. Rama Murthy	V.	State of Karnataka, AIR 1997 SC 1739
25. R.S. Sodhi	V.	State of U.P. 1994 Supp(1) SCC 142

26. State of Bihar	V.	Renahi Zila Samta Party AIR 1996 SC 1515
27. State of Bihar	V.	Union of India, AIR 1986 SC 1773
28. S.Jagannath	V.	Union of India, AIR 1997 SC 811
29. Sheonandan Paswan	V.	State of Bihar, AIR 1987 SC 877
30. Shiv Sagar Tewari	V.	Union of India, AIR 1997 SC 2725
31. T.N. Godawarman	V.	Union of India, AIR 1997 SC 1220
32. Tehri Bandh Virodhi Sangharsha Samiti	V.	State of U.P. 1992 Supp(1) SCC 44
33. Vineet Narayan	V.	Union of India, AIR 1996 SC 3386.